Devotions for Ministry Wives

~ *Barbara Hughes, Editor* ~

Devotions for Ministry Wives
Encouragement from Those Who've Been There

Foreword by Jill Briscoe

ZONDERVAN™

GRAND RAPIDS, MICHIGAN 49530 USA

Devotions for Ministry Wives
Copyright © 2002 by Barbara Hughes

Requests for information should be addressed to:
Zondervan, *Grand Rapids, Michigan 49530*

Library of Congress Cataloging-in-Publication Data

Devotions for ministry wives : encouragement from those who've been there /
Barbara Hughes, editor.
    p. cm.
  Includes index.
  ISBN 0-310-23632-0 (hardcover)
  1. Spouses of clergy — Prayer-books and devotions — English. 2. Wives —
Prayer-books and devotions — English. I. Hughes, Barbara.
  BV4395 .D45 2002
  242' .6435 — dc21

                                      2002000773

Interior design by Susan Ambs

Printed in the United States of America

07 08 /❖ DC/ 10 9 8 7 6

For Tricia

Beloved daughter-in-law,
pastor's wife, friend

Contents

Foreword

Dear Reader,

Here is sweet counsel, holy help, and wonderful wisdom from deeply committed women who have "been there." Where have they been? In the trenches of ministry at all levels. Here you will find a refreshing, positive look at serving Jesus.

Ministry carries with it a cost, yet it is an eminently worthwhile cost. Surely, these friends tell us, being a ministry wife is a privilege and not a punishment!

As editor of a magazine for ministry wives (*Just Between Us* [justbetweenus.org]), I hear the heartbeat of our high calling. After forty-five years in ministry—first as a layman's wife, then as a missionary wife, then as a pastor's wife, and now as a partner with my husband, commissioned to travel the globe to strengthen the arm of the church as ministers at large for Elmbrook Church (Milwaukee, Wisconsin)—I look back with a huge sense of gratitude for it all—but I wish I had had a book like this to cheer me on!

Many ministry wives find their hearts failing them for fear, and others wonder if they can face another day. Along with the privileged position we women have comes the challenge of learning what to do with loneliness, balancing family and ministry, dealing with private pain publicly, and coping with unrealistic expectations.

With the specific needs of ministry wives in mind, godly gifted partners have shared their words "aptly spoken." They are, as the Bible says in Proverbs

25:11, "like apples of gold in settings of silver." A bite of just "an apple a day" will surely keep the devil away!

God is good—all the time. God is so merciful and gracious. God is a very present help in trouble. Reach into the encouragement waiting in these pages, and find renewal and refreshment along the way—and the grace to go on. Happy reading!

—Jill Briscoe, Minister at Large, Elmbrook Church,
and editor of *Just Between Us*

Introduction

The question, "Will you marry me?" is one women have contemplated for centuries. But when the question is posed by a young man entering the Christian ministry, it presents a host of fears for the addressee:

- Will I fit the mold?
- Do I want to fit the mold?
- Do I have to fit the mold?!

Many a young woman has accepted such a marriage proposal in spite of her fears, only to be pleasantly surprised by the unexpected joys of serving Christ and his church. However, ministry wives do face unique challenges. This book addresses many of these particular stresses. The devotions are written by a sparkling array of authors who represent a marvelous diversity in ministry—missionaries' wives as well as pastors' wives, and wives of the presidents of Christian organizations and academic institutions. Some well-known names and some not so well-known, but all possessing a wealth of experience and unique gifts of expression:

- "It is not, as someone once quipped to me, 'a job that allows you a weeklong quiet-time.'"
- "Don't expect healthy responses from unhealthy people."
- "Sometimes we just can't fix what hurts in this world and in our churches."

These devotions cover a wide range of topics: personal discipline, dealing with criticism of your husband, feelings of inadequacy, facing unwelcome or unexpected changes in ministry, and the particular joys attendant to this privileged position:

- "Following God down his path is not always comfortable, but I believe it is only on this 'path of life' that I truly find joy and eternal pleasures!"
- "Our whole family has enjoyed making new friends, cultivating deep relationships, and cherishing precious memories. . . . We would have missed out on so much if we had allowed the deficiencies of our house to dictate the use of our home."

I began to look forward to the mail delivery each day as various authors sent me their contributions. I read and reread them—not for their literary form, but for my heart. Each woman's wisdom, gained through the application of God's Word to her day-in and day-out experience, lifted my heart in praise for the opportunity that is mine—and yours. I was encouraged to press on in this walk of faith and especially in my honored opportunity as a ministry wife.

My prayer is that each one of you who reads this book will be likewise encouraged.

Hallelujah! What a Savior!

Devotions for Ministry Wives

Encouragement from Those Who've Been There

1   **The Short End**

Barbara Hughes

Surely the arm of the LORD is not too short to save.

Isaiah 59:1

Short is something I understand. I'm short. My father was short, my mother is short, my siblings are short, and all my children—except for one—are short. We are well acquainted with the teasing that comes with being short—nicknames such as "Shorty," "Pee-wee," and "Shrimp-boat," and taunting songs such as "Short People Have No Reason to Live." The message is clear: Short is defective. But of course, the teasing has all been in good fun and has given us many good laughs.

The very first verse I memorized as a child points to another "short" that is far more serious in nature. "For all have sinned and fall short of the glory of God" (Romans 3:23). Even the tallest person has inherited this "short" gene and is seriously defective. No one laughs when they are called up short in some failure. For ministry wives this sinful defect can sometimes be embarrassingly public: a neglected responsibility, a harsh word, an ungrateful spirit.

Even the tallest person has inherited this "short" gene and is seriously defective.

When the prophet Isaiah wrote the verse on which I base this devotion, he made a simple statement about the adequacy of our God: He is able to save. Jeremiah 32:17 agrees: "Ah, Sovereign LORD, you have made the heavens and the earth by your great power and outstretched arm. Nothing is too hard for you."

Often when I am stretching for something just out of reach or when I've come up short, I am reminded of this wonderful truth.

Thank you, dear Lord, that your arm "is not too short to save." Forgive me when I fall short of your glory in thought and word and deed. Give me grace to grow in the stature that truly counts. Amen.

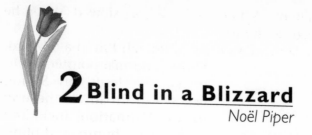

2 Blind in a Blizzard
Noël Piper

I will lead the blind by a way they do not know,
In paths they do not know I will guide them.
I will make darkness into light before them
And rugged places into plains.

Isaiah 42:16 NASB

I'd read in the *Little House* books about blizzards so thick you could get lost between house and barn. But I never thought blizzards like that happened to real people in real life.

My husband and I were driving home from a speaking engagement in South Dakota—across the prairie through a horizontal gale that was spray painting everything white. Centerline, shoulders, and ditches had disappeared. We couldn't pull off—we'd be buried in the snow and we'd freeze. Anyway, where was "off"? We surely didn't want to stop where another car could plow into us.

A semitrailer saved us. Its driver sat high, with the perspective to make out the snow bumps of signposts and other indicators of the road. We fell in behind him, thankfully and trustfully, our eyes glued to his lights. When he slowed, we slowed. When he swerved, so did we.

Some days I feel as though I'm in a blizzard, with all normal pointers obliterated. But Jesus, my Savior, can see my road all the way to my destination, including every curve, bump, and blind spot that confronts me today.

Jesus, my Savior, can see my road all the way to my destination.

In that prairie snowstorm, I had to keep my eyes on the semi and follow it; I didn't have any other choice if I wanted to avoid crashing. Every day we need to "fix our eyes on Jesus, the author and perfecter of our faith" (Hebrews 12:2) and follow him; we don't really have any other choice—besides crashing.

Dear Jesus, our Savior, please save me from today's blizzard. Fill my eyes and heart with you, so that I love to follow you. Amen.

3   The Sound of His Voice

Joyce Webster

> *When he has brought out all his own, he goes on ahead of them, and his sheep follow him because they know his voice.*

> *John 10:4*

"How about going to the movies with me tonight?" asked the young man on the other end of the phone. I gleefully accepted, knowing he was going to be in for a surprise when he realized to whom he was talking. Once again I had the fun of hearing one of my daughter's friends stammering for words when he discovered he had mistaken my voice for my daughter's—and had just asked her mother for a date.

When Jesus said "his sheep follow him because they know his voice," it shows the intimate relationship between us and our Shepherd. We need to know him so well that we are never fooled by impostors. There are many voices we hear that sound right but are not the ones we are meant to follow. I can be misled by these voices that sound so similar to God's.

24

As a woman in ministry I hear voices call me to good, compassionate, and caring actions. Who is it that tells me to start a new program at church, take a meal to a sick neighbor, be available for a hurting friend, care for my children, show my husband he is loved? How do I choose which actions to take, given the limitations on my time, energy, and abilities? I must distinguish God's voice from all others. The Bible is God's word to me. The distinctive sound of God's voice is recorded on my heart through his word. To confidently choose my actions I must be listening for the unique sound of my Shepherd's voice. Then I can set aside "good" actions for the "right" actions. It is in hearing him alone that I will find fulfillment in the good purposes he has for me. The better I know the Shepherd, the better I know his voice.

I must distinguish God's voice from all others.

Father, give me ears that are tuned to you alone. Give me discernment to know the difference between your whisperings to me and the blaring sounds of unmet needs that would drown out your voice. Call to me, and I will follow. Amen.

25

4 Revitalizing Your Marriage

Dorothy Kelley Patterson

Remember therefore from where you have fallen;
repent and do the first works.

Revelation 2:5 NKJV

Marriage brings the greatest joys and offers the most awesome challenges. Those in ministry live in a fishbowl with little privacy. We are to be examples, and we ought to be circumspect in how we live. All eyes follow us, and judgment is never far behind. Mistakes are magnified and good deeds minimized. Both you and your minister-husband are pulled in so many directions that you may end up giving your freshest creativity and first energies to the ministry, with leftovers for children and each other.

The formula for renewal is simple and adaptable to any relationship. First, you must remember why you chose one another in the beginning and how focused you were on each other's needs. What were the ingredients of your love? Then you must repent, that is, turn from the destructive path that leads away from loving intimacy, and determine to abandon the neglect and insensitivity that can lead

> *Both you and your minister-husband are pulled in so many directions.*

to a breakdown in your relationship. Finally, you must do the first works, returning to the acts of love that endeared you to one another in the first place. You must invest time, creativity, and energy in your marriage. When one partner pursues this commitment with passion, the other is pulled back to the center as well.

Heavenly Father, don't let me forget your priorities. Convict my heart and direct my will to remember the fruits of first love, and let your Spirit direct me away from neglect and indifference. Oh, that I might renew again the first works of love that will make my marriage strong and vibrant so that it enhances all I do in ministry. Amen.

5 The Climb to the Top

Kathy Chapell

He who dwells in the shelter of the Most High
    will rest in the shadow of the Almighty.
I will say of the LORD*, "He is my refuge and my*
        fortress,
    my God, in whom I trust."

Psalm 91:1–2

When our children were younger I often took them to a park where the main attraction was a large climbing structure of rough-hewn logs. One day our little Cori was determined to climb to the top. The timbers were huge compared to her small tender hands, and each rung of its ladderlike construction was an enormous step for her short little legs. Up she went, one rung, then the next, then the third—until she realized how high she was getting and called out for Mommy. I didn't want her to fall, so I climbed up behind her and put my hands beside each of her arms and my feet on the step just below her. I said, "Let's climb, Cori. I won't let you fall." Up we went, like a little spider covered by a big spider, and we made it to the top.

That is how God surrounds us as we climb through life. His arms are around us, and his sure and steady feet are beneath ours. He won't let us fall. At times we may feel that the climb is too steep for us and that the timbers are too rough under our hands. But God is always there, covering us with his love. God is big enough to take us to the top.

At times we may feel that the climb is too steep for us and that the timbers are too rough under our hands.

Father, just knowing that you are close to me gives me courage. Show me how to climb this path, and help me to feel your love covering me. Amen.

6
I'm Ugly
Jeanne Hendricks

He does not treat us as our sins deserve
or repay us according to our iniquities.
For as high as the heavens are above the earth,
so great is his love for those who fear him.
                                        Psalm 103:10–11

Liang was born in China without a complete facial structure. Her parents rejected her. Her grandmother sheltered her for a time but soon learned that the entire community had disowned this malformed little girl. Liang's grandmother made a decision to follow the local custom and leave Liang beside the road to die. Imagine Liang's thoughts: *I'm ugly. No one wants to look at me. I hate myself, and now I'm going to be thrown away because I'm worthless.*

The grandmother heard that an American doctor who could repair disfigured faces was coming to their village. Although she doubted that anything could help Liang, Grandmother would at least try. Today Liang is a walking miracle. She learned from the medical doctors that God loved her and gave the doctor the ability to make her face whole.

Then there's Kathy, who, though not out-wardly disfigured, hated herself inwardly. Late one

> *To have an older sister come alongside and assure them that God truly cares, and then show them where he says so in his Word, is the greatest gift they can get.*

night she called to tell me that she was about to take an over-dose of pills. I asked her to say it to God because God is infi-nitely more important than I am. She started to cry, and I gently quoted some verses of Scripture to assure her that she is worth much to him. Today Kathy works as a professional, but there are others, such as Marty, who heard the same negative messages and took their own lives.

Everywhere in our world there are young women bent on self-destruction, convinced they are useless and unimportant. To have an older sister come alongside and assure them that God truly cares, and then show them where he says so in his Word, is the greatest gift they can get.

Lord, open my mouth to speak your words of assurance to the many young women who stagger in self-contempt. Amen.

7   Pity the Pastor's Wife

Sue Sailhamer

> *I am sending you out like sheep among wolves.*
> *Therefore be as shrewd as snakes and as*
> *innocent as doves.*
>
> *Matthew 10:16*

Have you ever been reluctant to admit you were a pastor's wife? I sometimes bristle at the strange notions people attach to this misunderstood label.

In the early years of my marriage I attended a "neighborhood watch" meeting. We had just purchased our first home, and I thought it would be a great way to meet some new neighbors. My husband had a meeting at church that evening, so I went by myself. I returned home a sadder but wiser pastor's wife and neighbor.

That night I learned that a major feud was in progress on our block. Slashed tires and bricks thrown through windows were on the list of evil deeds returned for evil deeds. I remember my surprise at hearing what was going on behind the tranquil facade of the neatly groomed front yards on my street.

As I left the gathering a women asked me what my husband did. I told her he was a pastor, and I'll never forget her response. "Your poor little silver ears," she exclaimed. The woman was horrified that I had been exposed to the neighborhood gossip.

Her naive view that a pastor's wife is unaware of life's dirty little secrets couldn't be further from reality. On a daily basis pastors help people deal with the consequences of sin in their lives. And as pastors' wives we often carry these burdens with our husbands.

As pastors' wives we often carry these burdens with our husbands.

Over time I came to see that what really mattered was not what other people thought I was, but the joyful truth that *God knows who I am.* That is what matters.

Thank you, Lord, that you know me so well. Help me to be free from the trap of other people's false notions of who I am. Give me your grace to be the woman you would have me be. Amen.

8 Our Pilgrim Walk

Mary Lou Whitlock

> *Therefore, I urge you, brothers, in view of God's mercy, to offer your bodies as living sacrifices, holy and pleasing to God—this is your spiritual act of worship.*
>
> *Romans 12:1*

Bedford, England, the beautiful hometown of John Bunyan, is situated on the banks of the River Ouse. Visiting this lovely English town was a shot in the soul for me. As I walked around Bunyan's then and now famous church, I took in the beautiful stained-glass windows that depict major events in Bunyan's *The Pilgrim's Progress*. I recalled with great clarity his classic work and was struck again by the depth and persevering walk of this man's life.

After many years of spiritual unrest, in 1648 Bunyan began reading certain Christian books that belonged to his wife. Searching for answers to his questions, he finally received assurance of his salvation in 1653. Once he became a believer, preaching became his passion. Bunyan preached everywhere. In fact, Bunyan's preaching "outside" the established church landed him in prison. In prison Bunyan couldn't preach, but he could write—and that he did. Even today his great classic continues to minister to thousands of readers.

What lesson can we learn from this godly man? Prison walls cannot contain a man who has a passion to serve God. Bunyan didn't sit and plot ways—either legal or illegal—to escape the system. Instead, he turned to using his gifts in the best way possible for him at that time. No wasted hours. No wasted gifts. Bunyan used his gifts and passions according to the circumstances.

Prison walls cannot contain a man who has a passion to serve God.

Do we allow circumstances to hinder us from accomplishing our purpose to serve the Lord? Have our plans been waylaid by a person, a committee, a lack of funds or time, or perhaps a lack of initiative or motivation on our part. Satan would love for us to lose sight of our goals and purpose. Today, let's make every effort to serve our Savior with all of our resources.

Lord, help me to use all of my resources and all of my gifts to advance your purposes and bring glory to your name. Amen.

9   Eagles' Wings

Mary Kassian

You yourselves have seen what I did to Egypt, and how I carried you on eagles' wings and brought you to myself.

Exodus 19:4

Sometimes it feels as though God is not near. We look, but cannot see him. The children of Israel felt this way, too. They didn't see God supporting them when they suffered under their increased load (see Exodus 5:19–22). Nor did they see him when they were convinced they were going to die at the hands of the Egyptians or starve to death in the desert (see Exodus 14:10–12; 16:2–3). But the Lord loved to remind them, "I carried you on eagles' wings."

Have you ever wondered why God chose eagles as his metaphor to describe his actions? Eagles build nests at the tops of towering trees or high in rocky cliffs. When it is time for a young eaglet to fly, the parent coaxes it out to the edge of the nest and then pushes the eaglet off. If the eaglet refuses to come out, the parent stirs the nest and throws the eaglet out.

During this first flying lesson, the eaglet plunges hopelessly downward, flapping its wings in desperation. What the eaglet doesn't know is that the parent swoops down underneath it and flaps its own powerful wings. The updraft of air created by the parent's wings pushes the youngster up, enabling it to fly. Though unseen, the presence and strength and power of the parent guarantees that the eaglet won't be harmed.

"I carried you on eagles' wings."

God carries us on eagles' wings. When we feel as though we've been pushed out of the nest and are free-falling as we flap our wings in desperation, *God is there*—"carrying" us like an eagle. Though unseen, his strength and power are under us, bearing us up, protecting us, and enabling us to fly.

Dear Father, thank you for carrying me on eagles' wings. Thank you that I can trust your love, strength, and power to bear me up through the difficult circumstances and challenges of life. Teach me how to fly in the certainty of your abiding presence. Amen.

So the Next Generation Would Know

10

Jani Ortlund

*We will tell the next generation
the praiseworthy deeds of the LORD,
    his power, and the wonders he has done . . .
so the next generation would know them,
    even the children yet to be born,
    and they in turn would tell their children.*

Psalm 78:4, 6

As a child, I remember my Sunday school teachers at Lake Harriet Baptist Church—Miss Brown, Mrs. Hartill, Mrs. Berntsen. They faithfully taught me the power and wonders of the Lord Sunday after Sunday. The great biblical themes, the missionary stories, the memory work, and the eternal truths these women taught shaped my life—and consequently the lives of my children and grandchildren.

Don't miss the privilege of passing on the truth to the children in your church. Sunday school isn't glorified baby-sitting. It is the perfect opportunity to "tell the next generation the praiseworthy deeds of the LORD."

Resist the temptation to use your lack of knowledge or experience as an excuse. The children need you. If you have nothing to share, then come to God with your empty heart. Repent of your lack of intimacy with him. Ask him to reveal to you his wonders and powers and praiseworthy deeds. Then pass the truth along.

The eternal truths these women taught shaped my life—and consequently the lives of my children and grandchildren.

The next time the children of your church need someone to lead them, embrace the challenge. Any sacrifice you make will be worth it. As our son, Eric, wrote to us recently, "I guess sometimes you have to wait decades before some sacrifices pay off." But we serve the God who remembers (see Hebrews 6:10). Pass the truth along.

Father, I am ashamed of my dry and lazy heart. I want to change. Help me. Use my meager efforts to raise up strong faithful Christians for the coming years. In Jesus' name. Amen.

11   The Family Call

Paulette Washington

All this is from God, who reconciled us to himself through Christ and gave us the ministry of reconciliation.

2 Corinthians 5:18

All of us are called to be involved in the ministry of reconciliation, but some are gifted with a special call to be racial reconcilers. Recognizing God's call on my life to ministry was absolutely foundational to my husband's and my future ministry together. When I saw God's call on Raleigh's life to ministry, I was ecstatic to see what God was doing to prepare him for ministry. I wanted to do all I could to see Raleigh prepared.

In spite of all the hardships we faced in preparation for ministry, it was that sense of *call* that kept me going. It made the end in sight something tangible and completely founded on God's hand upon us.

Perhaps you've lost your sense of call to the ministry. Take some time today to go back and recall the time when you and your husband sensed

It was that sense of call

that kept me going.

God's call on you to ministry. It was no accident that Moses time and again recalled for the Israelites their history with God so that they could *do great things for God.* It strengthened their sense of calling to what God had for them.

There are times when we need to do the same thing—to recall and strengthen our own call to ministry. Take a look at what God has done in your lives as a result of that call. It could become a significant reminder not only of where you have been, but also of where God is taking you.

Heavenly Father, thank you for calling my husband and me to your work. Help me to remember and recall the way you've worked in the past in order that I may continue serving you today. Amen.

12 Hospitality Begins at Home

Mary K. Mohler

But if anyone does not provide for his own, and especially for those of his household, he has denied the faith and is worse than an unbeliever.

1 Timothy 5:8 NKJV

"Is that for people, or for us?" my hopeful eight-year-old daughter asked as I was putting the finishing touches on a chocolate cake. I was quite pleased to tell her that this time I made two cakes, and yes, there would be plenty for us.

My husband and I host over fifteen hundred guests in our home each year. Our children will grow up with memories of many wonderful occasions when guests graced our home. We want our children to learn to be gracious hosts themselves. Hospitality is a biblical command to all believers. However, I am mindful of the powerful message of 1 Timothy 5:8. It is wise to remember that *hospitality begins at home.* If we cannot make the precious family God has given us feel welcome, wanted, and unconditionally loved in their own home, we have absolutely no business opening our homes to others. If our families only see special food, table settings, and decor for company, then the message is clear: Company warrants special treatment; they don't. Furthermore, if our attitude is cheerful and pleasant only for guests but irritable and demanding when it's "just family," then we are sending a strong (and wrong) signal that comes through loud and clear.

Our children will grow up with memories of many wonderful occasions when guests graced our home.

Create an atmosphere that makes your family feel like royalty. Make memories. Cherish all the opportunities you have to prepare comfort foods. Your family members will be all the more willing to share the warmth of their home with company when they feel treasured themselves.

Lord, guard us as we reach out to others that we don't forget to reach out to those you have so graciously given us at home. In Jesus' name. Amen.

13 Discipline or Discouragement

Kathy Hicks

No discipline seems pleasant at the time, but painful. Later on, however, it produces a harvest of righteousness and peace for those who have been trained by it.

Hebrews 12:11

As a young woman I admired godly women speakers and wanted a ministry that would touch lives in the way they touched lives. Through the years I taught teen seminars and small group Bible studies when finally the opportunity came to speak at a mother-daughter conference. My friend and I were in charge of programming, and we felt that, between the two of us, we could handle the speaking. After all, the moms and their girls were mostly interested in being together. They didn't need a big-name speaker. So we shared the speaking.

The conference went all right—until we read the evaluations. Most were okay, but one singled me out and blasted me in a rather personal way. The evaluation listed "arrogance" and "being in need of spiritual renewal"—along with other criticisms. I was devastated. My friends assured me this woman was way off base and obviously had personal issues that I somehow had triggered. "Don't take it to heart," they said—but I did.

All real ministry only happens through God's power.

Was this God's discipline? Or was it Satan's discouragement? I swung between "I'll never be an effective speaker," and, "Lord, was she right? Were you speaking through her?"

Now I see that both Satan and God used the scathing evaluation. I allowed Satan to discourage me and keep me from trusting God in other opportunities. And God used it to humble and to teach me. As God brings other opportunities, this memory keeps me dependent on him, and aware that all real ministry only happens through his power.

Lord, thank you for your loving discipline that shapes me into someone who can be useful for your service. Thank you for the privilege of being a tool in your hand. Never let me forget that you are the one who accomplishes the work. Amen.

14 The Ministry of Hospitality

Heather Olford

Offer hospitality to one another without grumbling.

1 Peter 4:9

Have you ever realized how much the New Testament has to say about hospitality? Before using the home for hospitality, we must settle two questions: Is my home too humble for hospitality, or is it too extravagant?

Some homemakers are so house-proud that the very thought of entertaining visitors fills them with horror. What if someone breaks something? Or what if the rug gets stained? I like to take care of things in my home, but I would hate to become a slave to them so that I deny myself the fun and fellowship of entertaining guests. Some people may feel that they don't have all the right stuff to entertain in a way that guests would be favorably impressed. What we forget is that friends and guests do not look so much for material provisions as for spiritual welcome and fellowship.

They appreciate the sense of warmth and friendship in the home. Hospitality works in two ways. Not only do we bless and help those who visit, but we receive lasting benefits for ourselves and family.

Friends and guests do not look so much for material provisions as for spiritual welcome and fellowship.

Some of the deepest spiritual impressions from my childhood can be attributed to missionaries and preachers who came into my home. They were also strangers who turned out to be "angels" (see Hebrews 13:2). This was true in the Olford home when we were in our pastorates. We shared our home with many of God's servants, as well as with people in need of spiritual help. Both blessings and blessed!

Lord, make my home a haven to the stranger and a heaven to the saints, family, and friends for your glory. Amen.

15 Contentment at Home or Away

Lisa Ryken

Godliness with contentment is great gain.

1 Timothy 6:6

My father was an obstetrician and therefore did not work "normal" hours. He was frequently gone at unusual times of the day or night, much the same way a minister is. My husband works weekends. Sometimes he works early in the morning or late at night.

My mother, a very godly woman, gave me wonderful advice when she said, "Be content when he is at home and be content when he is away." This is an echo of Paul's exhortation in Philippians 4:11 to be content "whatever the circumstances." It's easy to become resentful and angry and then bitter with your husband—and with God—because of his work. When he has to make a hospital call or conduct an unexpected funeral, or when his sermon preparation takes longer than usual, do I respond with cheerful contentment or with grudging tolerance? One of my jobs as my husband's helper is to encourage him in his work.

What do I say to our children when they ask, "Where's Daddy?" My attitude usually determines how my children respond. If I'm angry about my husband's Saturday morning meeting, then my children are sure to be angry that Daddy can't be home to play with them. To be a godly mother and role model I need to respond to my children cheerfully. Instead of getting upset that my husband needs to go back to the office, I must pray that his work will be productive and joyful. This helps me to be content, to have a godly attitude, and to love my husband and his work.

> *It's easy to become resentful and angry and then bitter with your husband—and with God—because of his work.*

Lord, thank you for the work you have called my husband to do. I offer up my calling as a wife and mother as a gift to you today. Please forgive me for getting angry when work calls him. In all things may I be content. Amen.

16

Listening Is Golden

Barbara Hughes

Guard your steps when you go to the house of God. Go near to listen . . .

Ecclesiastes 5:1

Have you noticed how difficult it has become for people to listen? It's especially difficult to listen to the spoken word. And PowerPoint presentations that accompany most spoken words haven't helped matters. A flight attendant once addressed her Chicago-to-Cleveland flight: "When the oxygen mask drops down, apply firmly to your navel," and no one even looked up. Unaided and unhindered listening is golden.

God's Word instructs us to guard our steps when we go to God's house. It warns us to be careful to *listen*. Listening in church is hard when you're rushed or weary, distracted or bored. Nonetheless, we are to listen to the powerful Word of God as it is preached.

How blessed I am to be a ministry wife in this regard. Sunday after Sunday, month after month, year after year, I listen to my husband preach God's Word. And I listen more attentively to his words than anyone else in the congregation, because I love the preacher. I care about his delivery as well as about his message. I wince if he misspeaks or loses his train of thought. I pray that his words would be true and clear, and most of all, that they would be pleasing to God.

"When the oxygen mask drops down, apply firmly to your navel."

The benefits to me have been enormous. My mind is filled with God's Word. The Spirit of God has given me understanding beyond my natural ability because I have listened—and because I am married to the pastor.

Father God, thank you for this graced privilege. Now help me be a doer of the word and not just a hearer. Amen.

51

17 Say It to God

Noël Piper

He who dwells in the shelter of the Most High
Will abide in the shadow of the Almighty.
I will say to the LORD, "My refuge and my fortress,
My God, in whom I trust!"

Psalm 91:1–2 NASB

The biopsy is positive. She's terrified. I hang up the phone, concerned that my reassuring words were just words. Psalm 91 begins with the assurance I wanted to give: "... the shelter ... the shadow of the Almighty." And then the psalmist goes all the way praising God. He could have said, "The LORD is a refuge and a fortress." But that was too weak. He could have said, "The LORD is my refuge and my fortress." But that wasn't enough. He could have said something like I did to my friend: "The LORD will be your refuge and your fortress." It's true. But it's not enough.

The psalmist isn't even talking to *us*. He's talking to *God*.

I will say to the LORD,
"My refuge and my fortress,
My God, in whom I trust."

He can't lie to God. What he says to God is authentic and alive. If I say something to you about my relationship with God, I might make it look better than it really is. But not if I'm talking to God. I have to tell *him* the truth. So when the psalmist praises God *to* God, we believe that God *is* a refuge and fortress.

We believe that God is a refuge and fortress.

The next time my friend calls I want to assure her of "... the shelter ... the shadow of the Almighty." Then I will say *to the Lord* ....

O God, please forgive me for my empty words! Turn my mind and my mouth toward you, and may the truth that I speak to you be reassurance to someone who overhears. Amen.

18   The Sure Cure

Joyce Webster

> *Give thanks to the LORD, for he is good;
> his love endures forever.*
>
> 1 Chronicles 16:34

By now my pain had escalated to the point where I couldn't accomplish even the simplest tasks. I had been diagnosed with a chronic pain condition that could be treated but not cured. My daily hurdles were depression and inability to sleep well. The onset of these problems coincided exactly with the time of our new church-planting endeavor. At the very time I needed to encourage my husband and meet new people, I was finding myself depressed and discouraged. There seemed to be little evidence of God's presence in my life.

My daughter Joy gently reminded me of my own advice to her and her siblings. When one of them was discouraged, I would give them an uncomplicated prescription: Each morning they were to choose to begin the day with a large dose of gratitude.

They were to write down ten reasons for which they could be thankful to God, adding ten new reasons each day for at least a week.

My advice came back with a sting for me. I hate it when that happens! I now had to listen to my own counsel. I became acutely aware that this was not a simple treatment to take on. Nevertheless, once I started my list of reasons to be thankful, I began to notice a change, not in my physical condition, but in my heart attitude. Thankfulness administered faithfully to our hearts is a prescription for renewal. The importance of being thankful is clear through the repetitions of this instruction in God's Word.

Each morning they were to choose to begin the day with a large dose of gratitude.

Be thankful. Be thankful. Be thankful.

Lord, I don't always feel thankful. I don't always see the work you are continually carrying out on my behalf. Give me a clear vision to see the abundant reasons to possess a thankful heart. Amen.

19 Moving Through

Dorothy Kelley Patterson

When you pass through the waters,
I will be with you;
and when you pass through the rivers,
they will not sweep over you.
When you walk through the fire,
you will not be burned,
the flames will not set you ablaze.

Isaiah 43:2

On a small business card that had these verses printed on it, every *through* was underlined in red. The accompanying note reminded me of what it means to belong to the Lord.

When my husband was dismissed as president of a Bible college, it was an abrupt action. Under his leadership the institution had grown from twelve students to almost five hundred full-time students, from diplomas to fully accredited bachelor's and master's degrees, from being housed at a downtown church to having its own spacious campus. His firing seemed unfair. He had refused to abandon his passion for international missions and evangelism to assume a "CEO posture" of raising money and managing staff—and that refusal cost him the presidency. My husband's vision and calling hadn't changed, but the governing board had. And this came from church members and friends, not from pagan enemies. Although the board was forced by public opinion to rescind their action, we knew that our work was done. Yet God's moving us *through* took nine months.

How wonderful to know that he who will never betray and who will never fail is guiding you through!

Have you gone to church with pain in your heart and a lump in your throat? Have you tried to worship with tears of despair trickling down your cheeks? Has the joy you consistently experienced in worship turned to sorrow? Have the solicitous inquiries of "friends" deepened your wounds? How wonderful to know that he who will never betray and who will never fail is guiding you through!

Father, I have experienced indescribable joy ministering among the saints. I also know something of the pain you felt when one of your followers turned his back on you, ushering the enemy into the garden of intimacy. Thank you for bringing me through and for letting me drink from the cup of your suffering. Amen.

57

20   Inner Sickness
Kathy Chapell

My brothers, can a fig tree bear olives, or a grapevine bear figs? Neither can a salt spring produce fresh water.

James 3:12

Several years ago I had to struggle through the pain of what I felt was a friend's betrayal. My husband told me about some of the difficulties in this person's life, and then said, "Don't expect healthy responses from unhealthy people."

In life—and particularly in the ministry—we often deal with people who cause others pain. Some are, for whatever reason, not very kind people. But others are either in so much pain themselves or are so spiritually and emotionally crippled that their outward lives naturally reflect their inward struggles. I am often tempted to respond in anger to unfair and hurtful treatment from others, but then the Lord calls me to remember the anguish that this very sister or brother is in—and my own anger must melt away into compassion.

Here's an illustration of what I mean. Our youngest child has allergies. I don't enjoy waking up in the middle of the night to tend to her coughing attacks. Sometimes she coughs and sneezes on me, and I really don't like that. But I understand that her internal struggles outwardly affect others—especially me. Similarly, I can be understanding when my sister in Christ who, in her battles against besetting sins, is unkind to me or treats me unfairly. I don't have to like or approve of her actions in order to understand and to forgive the internal pain that causes them. When this is difficult to do, I pray that God will help me remember that *my* sins make me an unhealthy person whom Christ loves and forgives.

> *"Don't expect healthy responses from unhealthy people."*

Lord, help me to remember that you forgive my unhealthiness, and so I must also forgive those in my life who struggle with inner sickness. Grant me love and compassion, Lord, for your hurting children. Amen.

21

Turn Signal
Jeanne Hendricks

My times are in your hands.

Psalm 31:15a

The early years with four young children had been fun and busy, but now they were young teens who needed their own rooms and places for their endless stuff. *Lord,* I prayed, *this house is much too small, and you know how hard it is when we have guests. Everything is worn, and I'm really ashamed to invite friends here.* But hard as I tried, nothing changed. One day when everyone was gone, I walked through the house, and then fell on my knees by the living room sofa.

With tears, I told the Lord how disappointed I was with him. And as I waited, he told me how disappointed he was with *me* and my lack of gratitude. *All right, Lord,* I answered, *if I have to live here for the rest of my life, it's okay, but please change my heart and remove my bitter dissatisfaction.*

Two weeks later a real-estate friend accosted my husband at church and convinced him that he had found a house that would be perfect for our family. Whenever I had asked about house-hunting, my husband had always been too busy or not interested at the time, but now he agreed to go see it. It was just right, he said, but too expensive. He made what even our real-estate friend called a ridiculous offer. To our amazement the seller accepted, and then our own house sold in a short period of time.

With tears, I told the Lord how disappointed I was with him.

How much anxiety I would have avoided had I prayed that prayer sooner! I resolved then to practice a spirit of thanksgiving for everything and to make every effort to keep in step with God's timing.

Lord, in this confusing world, please help me to stay in close touch with you and to feel the pulse of your chronology. Amen.

22 Failure

Sue Sailhamer

Bring joy to your servant,
    for to you, O LORD,
    I lift up my soul.

You are forgiving and good, O LORD,
    abounding in love to all who call to you.
Hear my prayer, O LORD;
    listen to my cry for mercy.
In the day of my trouble I will call to you,
    for you will answer me.

Psalm 86:4–7

As the first year of my role as "mentor mom" in a Mothers of Preschoolers (MOPS) group at church came to an end, I met with the program coordinator to consider whether I should continue on into a second year. When she told me she felt there was something missing in my relationship with the group—that I had failed to connect—I was stunned.

A war of thoughts broke out in my head as I rationalized my friend's stinging comments. I was new to MOPS. Was I being unfairly compared to my predecessor, who had had three years to build relationships and gain experience as a mentor mom. Why hadn't anyone told me I was missing the mark?

As I thought and prayed the next day, I had to admit my friend was right. I had agreed to take on the ministry position with a halfhearted reluctance. Although I had spent considerable time administrating the program, I had failed to pursue personal involvement and hands-on mentoring. I had held back in an attempt to control my time. I had done things my way—and I had failed.

Failure can be God's greatest tool to turn our hearts toward him.

When our own failure confronts us, it's easy to run away, to make excuses, and to blame others. But the painful task of self-evaluation is ultimately our friend. Failure can be God's greatest tool to turn our hearts toward him.

It is through acknowledging our failures that we admit our total dependence on God's grace. My experience was a reminder that it is only through God's grace that we succeed at anything.

Forgive me, Father, for doing things my way and not your way. Thank you for your unfailing love. Help me to see clearly the path you want me to pursue. Amen.

23   **Pain and Joy**

Mary Lou Whitlock

*Consider it pure joy, my brothers, whenever you
face trials of many kinds.*

James 1:2

*Be this the purpose of my soul,
My solemn, my determined choice,
To yield to Thy supreme control
And in my every trial rejoice.*

Author Unknown

What's it like to stand at the just-bigger-than-a-shoebox casket of your infant daughter? Numbing. Surreal. The head and heart swirl—full of questions and no answers—as our twin baby girl was called back to our heavenly Father. Her identical twin sister struggled to live in an incubator.

It has been many years since my husband and I were players in that scene, but I can tell you that the intensity of the day lives in my heart forever. My hormones were raging. My body was still recovering from birth. And there were so many people to be concerned about—our other children, family members, friends, church members. *"O God, what do I do? Where do I start?"*

Somehow it all came down to one overriding thought: I am God's child. He had been faithful and loving in the past, and I must trust him now. I remember talking to my husband about peace, and we agreed that in this horrendous hurt, we felt God's presence, love, and peace. It was the work of the Holy Spirit. On my own I could not have felt the simultaneous pain and peace that I experienced. God's grace was sufficient.

On my own I could not have felt the simultaneous pain and peace that I experienced. God's grace was sufficient.

And so it was natural that I came to devour the words of Samuel Rutherford, a seventeenth-century man who stood strong for the Lord. During his ministry, Rutherford's first wife and two daughters died. In his second marriage, he and his wife had seven children. By the time Rutherford died, only one child survived—an eleven-year-old girl. How did Rutherford lighten the weight of his heart? He acknowledged that pain and joy were a part of Christ's plan for him and that sorrow and peace do indeed dwell side by side. It is a truth of living by faith.

65

Help us, heavenly Father, to see the work of your hand as your tender design for us. Amen.

24   **Build Your House**

Mary Kassian

*The wise woman builds her house,
   but with her own hands the foolish one
    tears hers down.*

Proverbs 14:1

      I recently redecorated my bedroom. I repainted the walls, hung a matching wallpaper border, refinished the furniture, and added new pictures and dried flower arrangements. It was a lot of work—but well worth it. I get a lot of satisfaction when I walk in the room and see the pretty decor.

      Generally speaking, it's the men who build the structures, and it's women who fill them with color, beauty, order, and life. It's women who make a house a home.

      Proverbs says that the wise woman builds her house. The Hebrew word for *build* means "to establish; to make firm or stable; to secure permanently." The word for *house* means "family." This verse draws a parallel between a woman's attention to the physical aspects of her home and her attention to her family's emotional and spiritual well-being. Just as a woman invests time, energy, and money into maintaining and beautifying her house, she ought to invest in building up the ones she loves. In doing so, she establishes her relationships, making them firm and stable.

This verse draws a parallel between a woman's attention to the physical aspects of her home and her attention to her family's emotional and spiritual well-being.

The foolish woman tears down her house with her own hands. Few of us would literally destroy our homes by slinging mud or smashing walls, yet sadly we don't think twice about emotionally smearing or assaulting our husbands and children. We bear grudges, bring up past hurts, sneer, belittle, or retaliate. This is foolish indeed.

Dear Father, forgive me for foolishly tearing down my house with my own hands. Help me to be wise. Help me to be careful to invest in building up those I love. Amen.

25 Proved Genuine

Jani Ortlund

These [trials] have come so that your faith—of greater worth than gold, which perishes even though refined by fire—may be proved genuine and may result in praise, glory and honor when Jesus Christ is revealed. Though you have not seen him, you love him; and even though you do not see him now, you believe in him and are filled with an inexpressible and glorious joy.

1 Peter 1:7–8

The note from my friend read in an all too familiar fashion: "My husband is resigning this Sunday. It's a long story, but the board asked him to. It has come as a complete shock to both of us. He will preach this Sunday and read his letter after the sermon. . . . One of the hard things for me will be teaching at VBS all next week while trying to handle my grief."

Who of us in ministry hasn't been wounded in one way or another? The trials we encounter have a purpose. God puts you into the refiner's fire in order to prove you. God is proving to you that your devotion to him is authentic. Each grief you bear purifies you. It burns out your natural superficiality. As my own dear husband, Ray, has told me, "Suffering validates our faith."

There we learn to need Jesus so much that we humble ourselves into his joy— a joy so grand that it exceeds the power of human expression: "[We] are filled with an inexpressible and glorious joy" (1 Peter 1:8). That is a taste of heaven right here on earth.

"Suffering validates our faith."

Dear sister, stay in the fire—don't run. Open your heart to the joy of God. Trust him. Taste him.

Dear Father, teach me to love you more than my own ideals, treasures, and reputation. Validate my faith. Prove me to be genuine. And as I trust in you, open my heart to taste your joys. In Jesus' name. Amen.

26 Commitment to Relationship

Paulette Washington

> *. . . your people will be my people and your God
> my God.*
>
> *Ruth 1:16*

The foundation to peace itself is a commitment to relationship. As a wife, the success of my husband comes when I am committed to my marriage to such a degree that his call is my call, his pain is my pain, and his joy is my joy. This is true because we are truly one. With this perspective, my husband is given freedom and can respond above and beyond the call of duty.

I am committed to our calling to ministry. When Raleigh was in seminary, he took a homiletics class. As a seminary wife, I could audit classes, so I audited this one. I did this not because I knew then what I would later come to recognize—that God had given me the gift of public speaking. I was doing it so I could learn all of the elements of putting a sermon together homiletically—so I could be my husband's best critic, encourager, and helper.

Over the years I have come to understand God's gift for me in this area. Raleigh and I frequently speak together. We do team sermons together. My joy is not only great but also overwhelming because of what God is doing in and through us together in ministry.

> I didn't go into this in order to get my fair share. I went into it to complement my husband.

What is important to understand is that I didn't go into this in order to get my fair share. I went into it to complement my husband and to do whatever it takes to ensure that he could be all that God desires for him. As I did this, Raleigh not only responded, but he has become God's instrument in helping me to become all that God has called me to be.

Father, keep my commitment to my marriage and to my husband's call to serve you—and above all, my commitment to you—strong and sure till the end. Thank you for your calling in our lives. May all that we do be for your glory. Amen.

27 Redeem the Time

Mary K. Mohler

> *See then that you walk circumspectly, not as fools but as wise, redeeming the time, because the days are evil.*
>
> *Ephesians 5:15–16 NKJV*

Sometimes I feel as though I'm being pulled by the hand, my hair blowing behind me as in a wind tunnel. It's almost as though I'm living in a fast-forward mode with scenes passing by at record speed. I am still in my thirties, yet days, months, and years fly by, especially when I look at the faces of my children.

Our lives are a mere blip on the world's radar screen. We want to make a lasting impact for the cause of Christ. We can recite names of ministry wives from history who have made significant contributions, women from Katharina Luther to Susanna Wesley to Sarah Edwards to Susannah Spurgeon, to name just a few. Countless others have made a profound impact, although few people would recognize their names.

God has purposely placed women in our lives whom we can mentor and influence for a season. There are opportunities for kingdom advancement all around us. How tragic when we let these opportunities slip by! If God grants us length of days, we will have the joy of sitting in our rocking chairs to reflect on our lives. Will you regret that you were too busy to redeem the time? Did you let disorganization and misplaced priorities limit your availability? *Today* is the day to resolve to make changes, with the Lord's help.

Our lives are a mere blip on the world's radar screen. We want to make a lasting impact for the cause of Christ.

What will history record about your pilgrimage as a ministry wife? Think about what you want your legacy to look like. Pray about how you can take steps toward achieving what the Lord wants you to do—and then redeem the time and do it.

Lord, let us be wise even today to use whatever circumstances come our way to be tasks undertaken for you. In Jesus' name. Amen.

28 Appointment Time

Kathy Hicks

There is an appointed time for everything. And there is a time for every event under heaven.

Ecclesiastes 3:1 NASB

We have a little lake behind our house. This spring we've watched two goslings grow up before our eyes. They've grown from balls of fuzzy yellow fluff—following closely behind mama goose, with papa goose on guard nearby—to becoming more independent. Now they scurry off in the grass to feed, while their mama and papa follow behind, still keeping an eye out for danger.

Watching the constant care and supervision these Canada geese provide for their young reminds me of another season of my life when my daughter was a toddler. My life was full of caring for her needs. She was the main focus of my days. I am particularly nostalgic about my baby girl as I enter a new season of life—my daughter heading off to college on the other side of the country. Since she is our only child, this leaves us with the proverbial empty nest. We are embarking into new territory, where we're not sure how often we'll get to see her, how we'll all handle the separation, or if she'll ever be back to live with us again.

Since she is our only child, this leaves us with the proverbial empty nest.

But I do know this: Although we don't know what the future holds, God does. And just as he's led us through all the previous seasons and changes in our lives, he'll guide us through this one, too. He'll provide strength, wisdom, and fulfillment as we depend on him and follow his lead.

Faithful Father, thank you that in the midst of change, you are unchanging. You are my rock and my comforter, my ever-present help in time of need. Amen.

29   **Christ Is All**

Heather Olford

. . . in all things [Christ] may have the preeminence.

Colossians 1:18 NKJV

The book of Colossians teaches that our Lord Jesus Christ is the preeminent one and the head of the church. We worship him because he deserves all of our allegiance and our love. We sing, "He is Lord"; but is he truly *Lord*? Remember, Jesus is Lord *of* all, or not Lord *at* all. It is a contradiction in terms to say that Jesus is Lord of part of my life. He must be Lord of *all!*

We agree that first things must be first in our lives, but how many of us, if we carefully examined our hearts, would find that often the truly important things in life are last, and the least important things are right up there in first place.

More and more we need to realize that we have been saved for two great purposes in life—the first is to *worship,* and the second is to *witness.* If you and I are not a worshiping people, then the witness of our lives will be weak and fruitless. There are two aspects of worship that are vital. The first is the personal quiet place of communion with God. This is where we spend time in praise, adoration, and thankfulness for all that God is and for all that our preeminent Lord Jesus has done for us. The second crucial aspect is our public worship, where we join with fellow believers in church and together worship God. Never treat public worship lightly.

Never treat public worship lightly.

Out of worship flows our witness. If Christ is preeminent in our hearts then "out of the overflow of the heart the mouth speaks" (Matthew 12:34). When Christ is Lord of all, the Holy Spirit fills our lives, and we can't help but overflow in witness (see John 7:38–39).

Dear heavenly Father, you have exalted your Son, Jesus, to be both Lord and Christ. Can I do anything less? I pray that he may have preeminence in every area of my life for his name's sake. Amen.

30 Waiting on God

Lisa Ryken

Wait for the LORD;
be strong and take heart
and wait for the LORD.

Psalm 27:14

I spend much of my time waiting. I wait for children to come out of school or finish baseball practice. I wait for my husband to finish up one more thing in his study. I wait for the dryer repairman to come. I've waited for things that were out of my control—the birth of a child and job decisions that had to be made. These circumstances can be frustrating, but they remind me to wait for God.

When I became a minister's wife, a friend gave me Andrew Murray's book *Waiting on God*. It is a profoundly helpful book that has provided a wealth of encouragement and challenge. The idea of *waiting* is a recurring biblical theme, particularly in the psalms. We need to wait for God in so many ways and for so many things. Waiting forces us to sit before God in silence, without murmuring, and to worship him. We need to wait in hope—with anticipation and with thanksgiving. We need to wait for God to supply our needs and to give us his wisdom. We need to wait patiently.

Ultimately, waiting for God means trusting his sovereignty. When we wait for God, we no longer have to be agitated about situations beyond our control. Instead, we can be silent before God, restful and at peace. We can eagerly watch for what God is going to do. Waiting for God allows us to pray rather than worry and gives us hope that God will do above and beyond anything we can ask or imagine.

Waiting forces us to sit before God in silence, without murmuring, and to worship him.

Lord, you command us to wait for you. Please teach us how to wait, and give us joy in waiting for you. Amen.

31   **Upside Down**

Barbara Hughes

Love your enemies and pray for those who persecute you.

Matthew 5:44

Jesus always turns things on their head. His words grab our attention because they are out of sync with our inclinations. As a pastor's wife, one of the most liberating truths I have learned is found in Jesus' words, "Love your enemies and pray for those who persecute you."

When I began in ministry, I thought my enemies would be people outside the church—enemies of God and haters of the church. Sometimes they are, but far more often my enemies have been church members who worship alongside me and are, for one reason or another, opposed to my husband's leadership. These people *feel* like enemies. Sometimes they truly are.

Generally my response had been to give in to my natural inclination toward resentment and anger.

But anger saps strength and wastes energy. If anger takes root in your heart, it can get a deep-seated stranglehold. That is what happened to me.

One day Jesus began to carry out some serious surgery on my ugly attitudes. Taking Jesus at his word, I began to pray for my enemies. And I didn't simply pray feebly that God would "bless" them. I prayed fervently. I prayed the same things for them that I prayed for my children. Good things. Scriptural blessings.

When I began in ministry, I thought my enemies would be people outside the church.

And as I prayed, the Lord began to snip away at the anger and resentment that had filled my heart and allowed genuine, heartfelt love to fill the space.

Lord Jesus, please help me always to behave as a child of God, not giving in to my natural inclinations. Thank you that obedience liberates me. Your words are true. They cut away the ugly and make me beautiful. O Lord, I love you! Amen.

32 Not Ready to Be Blessed

Noël Piper

The LORD longs to be gracious to you,
And therefore He waits on high to have
compassion on you.
For the LORD is a God of justice;
How blessed are all those who long for Him.

Isaiah 30:18 NASB

Even in the face of freshman insecurities, I confidently declared, "I'll never marry a preacher!" For starters, I wasn't good enough, and besides, it wouldn't be fun. And I knew the value of fun.

Soon I met my future husband—a pre-med student. That suited me. But then he decided to study the Bible, so he was going to be headed to seminary. This was "dangerous" territory. But God's choice of a good husband was more important to me than possible career moves. Anyway, he planned to be a teacher, not a preacher, and that suited me.

After he completed his education, he taught Bible at a Christian college. God's gracious gifts through those years—of births and deaths, health and illness, pain and peace—proved that fun wasn't the measure of everything. It was *God* I wanted—God and his ways.

One morning my husband asked, "What would you think if I became a pastor?" If he became a pastor, I'd be married to a preacher. That suited me—"I've seen this coming for a long time. I'll be happy with whatever God leads you to do."

"I'll never marry a preacher!"

From the day of my foolish freshman pronouncement until the morning of that life-changing question, God waited fifteen years. He spent fifteen years reshaping my heart, making me willing to be blessed with the life he had waiting for me—life as a pastor's wife.

Compassionate Father, please keep reshaping me so that I want you and that I love the plans you have for me. Thank you that your plans for me are good and that they will give me a future and a hope. Amen.

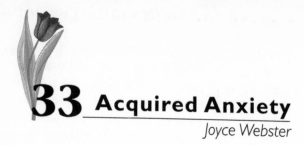

33 Acquired Anxiety

Joyce Webster

Cast all your anxiety on him because he cares for you.

1 Peter 5:7

When we moved to the United States from Europe, we brought very little with us. Believe it or not, the joy of shopping soon lost its appeal as we confronted the overwhelming task of setting up our new home. When we were planning our move, we thought it sounded like fun to be able to go out and buy everything we would need. The actual doing of it was daunting. As a responsible Christian mother and wife, I knew it was important to stay within our budget and still create a comfortable, inviting home. But the need to economically and sensibly outfit our home created anxiety for me. Afraid of making a bad decision, I began to avoid making any decisions at all.

Questions began to flood my mind: How could I spend so much time, energy, and money on acquiring material possessions? Why would God possibly care about the color of my kitchen dishes or the fabric choice of my new sofa? Wasn't my focus on the temporal getting in the way of my praying about the really important issues in the world? While the decisions about my house were significant for me, I couldn't see how they could be significant to God.

Then I began to focus on God's feelings toward me. He loves *me*. He cares about *me*. My anxiety eased when I recognized that God *did* care about my kitchen dishes and my sofa, not because those are such momentous issues to him but because they were significant to me—and he cares for me! As I sought God's direction concerning the mundane details involved in setting up our new home, I also developed a new sense of God's personal concern for me. He not only helped me make good decisions, he turned my heart toward him as well. Anxiety is eased when I possess faith in God's care for me.

Anxiety is eased when I possess faith in God's care for me.

Lord, thank you for caring for me. Thank you for caring about anything that creates anxiety within me. Help me use my anxious thoughts as an opportunity to trust you more fully and to experience your care in fresh ways. Amen.

34   Yet I Will Praise Him

Dorothy Kelley Patterson

> *Why are you downcast, O my soul?*
> *Why so disturbed within me?*
> *Put your hope in God,*
>   *for I will yet praise him,*
>   *my Savior and my God.*

Psalm 42:11

What ministry wife hasn't experienced the act of pursuing God with all her heart—serving her husband, nurturing her children, working in the church—and all the while her world is falling apart? Psalm 42 is the heart cry of one who struggled with doubts and depression.

During a family crisis, I agonized before the Lord. I prayed for a quick solution. I thought of ways to solve the problem. My thoughts and energies centered on my family tragedy—but God was silent.

In my anguish I asked my husband to cancel an upcoming engagement for me. I felt physically ill and emotionally drained. The last thing I wanted to do was teach a seminar. My husband wouldn't make the call, but he gave me permission to cancel the event. Since I wasn't "too sick" to make the call myself, I decided to go to the seminar, carrying my burden and grief with me.

A banner hung over the church platform: GOD STILL MOVES. A familiar chorus was being sung: "God still moves! God still moves! In the hearts of his people God still moves! He neither sleeps nor does he slumber. God still moves! God still moves!" Quickly I turned to Psalm 42, to the Lord's song in the night for my pain and anguish: "Put your hope in God, for I will yet praise him."

My thoughts and energies centered on my family tragedy—but God was silent.

Heavenly Father, other tragedies and challenges have come. I have claimed this promise often, knowing that even if I do not see the problem resolved on my timetable or in my lifetime, I can still rest in you—yet I will praise you! Amen.

35   Locked Up

Kathy Chapell

*"Their sins and lawless acts
I will remember no more."*

*And where these have been forgiven, there is no
longer any sacrifice for sin.*

Hebrews 10:17–18

Satan is very crafty, you know. He often haunts us with the sins of our past—reminding us over and over of those cruel words we spoke, the times we rebelled against God, the opportunities for ministry we deliberately ignored. At one point in my life the weight of these guilt-laden memories began to crush me and to cripple even my ability to feel the love of God.

In a desperate effort to throw off this relentless guilt, I finally began to pray, "Lord, don't let me remember that anymore. Take away even the memory of that sin. Lock it up, Lord, somewhere where I can't find it anymore." And God in his grace began to heal me.

Here's a mental picture that has helped me. In my mind's eye I see a file cabinet—a very strong cabinet capable of being locked. In the drawers are the files containing the records—the memories—

The key is in Christ's hand.

of my stupid, thoughtless, and weak failures. The drawers are shut tightly, and they are locked. And the key is in Christ's hand—his blood-stained, nail-pierced hand. I can't open those drawers anymore. Christ's sacrifice has closed them once and for all.

Sometimes Satan still tries to taunt me and remind me how weak I am and how weak I've been. When I feel those insidious barbs begin to prick my heart, I picture my locked file of tears, and I turn my back on the Evil One and cling instead to the hands that hold my salvation.

Dear Father, thank you for canceling the debt of my sin. Now help me to remember, day by day, that your cleansing blood also wipes away the guilt I still feel. Fill me instead with your love and peace, dear Father. Amen.

36 Blind Alley

Jeanne Hendricks

> *I lie down and sleep;*
> *   I wake again, because the LORD sustains me.*
> *I will not fear . . .*
>
> *Psalm 3:5–6a*

The plane landed, and we were there to meet Daddy—but he wasn't on the flight. I tried to explain to my little children that Jesus knew where Daddy was—even though we didn't—but my own heart was in turmoil. We got back home, I put them to bed calmly, and then I fell apart in my bedroom. My husband always called if plans changed, so I dialed the phone number of the place where he had been, and the custodian assured me that all the speakers had left the building together and had headed for the airport.

Something terrible must have happened, but it was late at night and what could I do? In a panic, I knelt next to the bed and shuffled through my Bible. I zeroed in on Psalm 3 and the phrase "I lie down and sleep," and my reaction was one of anger.

I thought, *God, don't play games with me! How can I sleep?* But there it was, so I took him up on it and got into bed.

It was 4:00 A.M. when the phone rang. I picked it up and heard my husband's voice: "Could you possibly come and pick me up at the airport?" My husband's flight had had engine problems and had landed at an obscure airfield without a telephone, so he was delayed until he could board a later flight to Dallas.

> *I put them to bed calmly, and then I fell apart in my bedroom.*

And the Lord said to me, "Don't you remember? He's mine, and I will take care of him."

Dear Father, help me always to trust you with those I love, because your watchful care is totally reliable. In Jesus' name. Amen.

37 Dream House

Sue Sailhamer

Unless the Lord builds the house,
its builders labor in vain.

Psalm 127:1a

For many years I admired one particular house in my neighborhood. An expansive front yard and two large shade trees added country charm to the old-fashioned yellow house with green shutters.

What did it look like on the inside? I wondered. I loved the curb appeal of the staggered brick steps that led to the front door. I once mustered up the courage to ring the doorbell and ask who laid the brick and concrete for the inviting walkway, as our front path was in need of repair.

I watched carefully when workmen added a second story. A few years later the bigger and better version of my dream house went up for sale. I was told it was because the owners got divorced.

A number of years have now passed, and I finally met the woman who lives in my favorite yellow house. She satisfied my curiosity with a tour of her home's remodeled interior. As details from her ailing marriage spilled out, I couldn't help but sense the contrast between the visible image of her lovely home and the invisible pain within her heart.

> I couldn't help but sense the contrast between the visible image of her lovely home and the invisible pain within her heart.

The encounter with my new friend was a powerful reminder that looks can be deceiving. What value do beautiful new furniture and great landscaping have when there is no love between husband and wife?

I want to fashion my house according to God's plan. My home may not look like a dream house, but if I build it God's way, it will be the house of my dreams.

Lord, thank you that *you* are the master builder and have provided the blueprint for me to build my home according to your plan. Help me seek your truths rather than the latest fad that will ultimately fade and can never bring satisfaction. Amen.

38 How Are Things at Church?

Mary Lou Whitlock

> *To the saints in Ephesus, the faithful in Christ Jesus: Grace and peace to you from God our Father and the Lord Jesus Christ.*
>
> *Ephesians 1:1–2*

> *I thank my God every time I remember you. In all my prayers for all of you, I always pray with joy.*
>
> *Philippians 1:3–4*

Peruse the salutations and opening remarks Paul writes to the churches in Ephesus and Philippi. If Paul were writing to your church or mine, I wonder what his greeting would be? Has the testimony of our church advanced miles away? Has our church become known as a place where the saints of God come together and worship? Would we be called beloved, one in Christ, united? Would we be known for bearing one another's burdens and caring for each other?

In the dark days of personal loss, our family received great love and a united effort of the body of

Christ when our infant daughter went home to heaven. This baby was one of identical twins born prematurely. Our other baby's life hung by a thin thread. I had witnessed unity before, but now I saw mighty prayer and the circle of believers literally lift us from grief and fear. We were the ministers, but we were ministered to, blessed, and comforted by those who make up the family of faith.

I saw mighty prayer and the circle of believers literally lift us from grief and fear.

On how many other occasions have the compassionate words and actions of fellow believers helped sustain us? I ask this question not only for me but also for you. The thoughtfulness of a phone call, a visit, an encouraging word, a gift of food, a supporting shoulder—all of which has made an incredible difference in bearing our burdens. Let's thank God today for those he brings into our lives as his ministering angels.

Our loving heavenly Father, only you know how to give us just what we need. Thank you for always showing mercy and love, grace and compassion, when we are needy. Help us to appreciate both the gifts and the givers you provide. Amen.

39   **Little Things**

Mary Kassian

Catch for us the foxes,
   the little foxes
that ruin the vineyards,
   our vineyards that are in bloom.

My lover is mine and I am his. . . .

                      Song of Songs 2:15–16a

Have you ever noticed that it's the little things, not the big disasters, that do the most damage? The slow drip of water from the tap discolors the bathtub. The table surface is marred because the coffee spill wasn't immediately wiped up.

It's the "little foxes that ruin the vineyards." This is particularly true when it comes to relationships, as the beloved in Solomon's Song of Songs observes. The snappy reply, the small irritation, the hug not given—all these little foxes threaten to destroy the beauty of a vineyard in bloom.

It's important that I take care to "catch" the little things that damage my relationships. In terms of my relationship with God, I can't afford to neglect prayer, repentance, time with God, and the gentle guidance of the Holy Spirit. As a wife, I need to attend to the little things in my marriage, such as expressing appreciation and affection. It's a woman's capacity to notice and attend to the little things that make a house a place of refuge and rest.

The beloved gives the reason for her concern about the little foxes: "My lover is mine and I am his." It is her commitment to *unity* and *intimacy* that motivates her concern. She knows that intimacy is cultivated and maintained in the details. It is the little foxes, not the huge dragons, that pose the greatest threat to her. Consider your most important relationships—God, your husband, your children, your friends. Are there any little foxes you need to catch today?

> It's important that I take care to "catch" the little things that damage my relationships.

Dear Father, help me catch the little foxes that can ruin the beauty of the vineyards of my relationships. Help me avoid neglecting the small things that are necessary to cultivate in order to maintain unity and intimacy with you and with those you have graciously placed in my life. Amen.

Protection against the Storms

Jani Ortlund

Then they cried out to the LORD in their trouble,
and he brought them out of their distress.
He stilled the storm to a whisper;
the waves of the sea were hushed.

Psalm 107:28–29

A few years ago the basement of our home flooded during a violent storm. As Ray and I waded through the muck, I was dismayed to see the box in which my wedding dress had been stored floating in that filthy water. Too disheartened to open the box, I tossed it on top of our Ping-Pong table and carried on with the cleanup.

Several days later I mustered up the courage to assess the damage to this sentimental treasure. As I removed the mud-caked lid, I was surprised to discover that only a minimal amount of silt had seeped through the well-sealed plastic bag. My gown had been sealed securely by layers of waterproof materials and was completely untouched by all the filth and water in which it had been floating.

It's the same for your soul. It must be protected against the storms of life. A life devoted to ministry will encounter furious storms that come up without warning—the staff member caught in adultery, the slanderous rumor about your husband, the onset of sudden illness. What protects your soul day after day?

I was dismayed to see the box in which my wedding dress had been stored floating in that filthy water.

God wants to be your daily security. Hold fast to him (see Joshua 22:5). Put all your trust in him. Nurture your inner life. Rest in the assurances of God's Word. Visit the throne of grace often (see Hebrews 4:16). Let your soul find rest in God alone (see Psalm 62:1). Layer your soul against the storms of life.

Lord, sometimes I feel like crying, as the disciples did in the midst of their storm, "Lord, save us! We're going to drown!" When my storms rage, increase my faith. Quiet my heart. Bring me to a place of quiet rest. Calm my storm to a whisper. In Jesus' name. Amen.

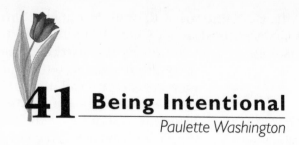

41 Being Intentional

Paulette Washington

For he himself is our peace, who has made the two one and has destroyed the barrier, the dividing wall of hostility.

Ephesians 2:14

Nothing happens if you're not intentional about it. The reality is that we are intentional in *everything* we do. We may not be aware of what our intentions are, but we still make decisions about what we do.

The burden of my heart is for reconciliation and diversity. I have to realize and believe that we need to be intentional in reaching out to women who are different from us. That's a real stretch, considering the wounds and hurts we've often suffered as ministry wives. In spite of that, however, we are not released from being a part of others' lives, confident that God will provide for our needs and heal our hurts.

We need to be thinking of diversity and reconciliation in our ministries to others. We can lead the way in modeling the kind of intentionality that reflects God's purposeful activity in bringing us into relationship with him. It starts with reaching out to women who are different from us—whether a different race, different denomination, or different social status.

I have to realize and believe that we need to be intentional in reaching out to women who are different from us.

Ask yourself, What am I doing? Do I spend more time protecting myself from others than reaching out to them? God has prepared and placed you in the ministry, as was true for Esther, "for such a time as this" (Esther 4:14). Dare to discover what your role can be in the lives of others who are distinctly different from you, and then move with confidence toward living it out.

God, through your Son you broke down the barriers that separate people. Help me to be intentional in crossing the lines of race and social status as I build my relationships. Amen.

42   A Heart That's His

Mary K. Mohler

For the eyes of the LORD move to and fro throughout the earth that He may strongly support those whose heart is completely His.

2 Chronicles 16:9a NASB

At some point in your pilgrimage as a ministry wife you have undoubtedly been asked the question, "Do you play the piano?" There are certain stereotypes that tend to follow ministry wives. One of the courses I teach to seminary student wives addresses the issue of our calling. We list as many stereotypical traits of pastors' wives as we can come up with. When the list is complete, some class members proclaim, "I don't have a single one of those traits!" As much as we want to be equipped to serve, we must be quick to realize that there is no mold we must fit.

Have you ever questioned your calling? Some ministry wives struggle with the idea that their husbands were called—but perhaps they were not. Think about this. Before the foundation of the universe, our sovereign God knew that your husband would answer the call to ministry. Furthermore, God knew that you would marry that man. So God has been preparing you all your life to be not only your husband's helpmate but his partner in ministry as well.

We list as many stereotypical traits of pastors' wives as we can come up with.

God did not call you to be someone you are not. He wants you to be the woman he created for a special purpose at this particular time in history in order to accomplish his work and bring him glory. That's good news. The only qualification that should be on our list is a desire to be teachable as we seek the Lord with all our hearts.

Father, it is so awesome to realize that you are actively seeking those people whose hearts are completely yours. We long to be those people. Grant us the desire, the discipline, and the commitment to do so. In Jesus' name. Amen.

43

Ultimate Power Source

Kathy Hicks

But the fruit of the Spirit is love, joy, peace, patience, kindness, goodness, faithfulness, gentleness and self-control. Against such things there is no law.

Galatians 5:22–23

Being a woman in ministry is exhilarating and exhausting at the same time—so many opportunities, so many needs, so many demands. Sometimes I'm overwhelmed by the privilege, and other times I'm overwhelmed by the responsibility and the schedule. The only way to cope is by plugging into the ultimate power source—the power of the Holy Spirit.

Sometimes I fall back on my own power sources—my batteries of hard work, good intentions, not wanting to fail my husband or the Lord, or just being too proud to allow myself to fail. I can get along for a while on these batteries, but eventually they wear out, and so do I. It's times like these when I use the fruit of the Spirit as a "power source check." Is my heart missing joy or peace? Am I out of control or being unkind? Is my motivation love, or is it some-thing less honorable? If the fruit is missing, I know I'm not plugged into God's power but trying to get along on my own. Then I know it's time to confess my self-sufficiency (which isn't sufficient at all!) and return to God-dependency. I can do all things through Christ who strengthens me—but only if I let him!

Being a woman in ministry is exhilarating and exhausting at the same time.

Patient Father, forgive me for the times I launch out to try to serve you in my own strength. Keep me mindful that only what is accomplished through your power has any lasting value or impact. Remind me to be a "fruit inspector" so I will know when I'm not living by the power of your Spirit. Amen.

44 The Virtuous Woman

Heather Olford

*Who can find a virtuous woman? for her price is
far above rubies.*

Proverbs 31:10 KJV

Women are featured often in the Bible. In
fact, we could, if we wanted to, spend all of our time
studying their lives. To me Proverbs 31:10–31 says it
all. Why? Because it presents God's standard for all
women. Please read these verses personally and
prayerfully.

Did you notice that at least four parts of a
woman's body are alluded to in this passage? Her
hands (31:13, 19) are used for God, her family, and
her neighbors. As a worker she takes delight in all she
does. Her *eyes* (31:16, 18, 27) see opportunities in the
home and beyond. Her *mouth* (31:26) speaks wisdom
every time she opens it. What a blessing to be able to
use our mouths to give wisdom and guidance! Then,
very important, is her *heart* (31:11, 30), which is loyal
to her husband and family and faithful to her Lord.

Proverbs 31:10–31 becomes a glorious standard and guide to living a life of purity and praise. In these days of low standards that affect every aspect of life, it's wonderful to be able to turn to God's Word, which not only has rules and standards, but the right ones—as well as the secret of where we get the strength to keep them.

Proverbs 31:10–31 becomes a glorious standard and guide to living a life of purity and praise.

The challenge from this passage to you and me is the challenge of a life of true virtue and praise. Purity represents the horizontal relationships, while praise represents the vertical relationship. Day by day we must claim the power of the Holy Spirit to control our relationships so that we can live out the Christ-life in purity and praise.

Dear Lord, take my life and let it be consecrated, Lord, to Thee. (Frances R. Havergal) Help me to be virtuous as a woman, a wife, a mother, and a servant of God. I pray in Jesus' name. Amen.

45   **Bride of Christ**

Lisa Ryken

> *My lover is radiant and ruddy,*
>   *outstanding among ten thousand. . . .*
>
> *His mouth is sweetness itself;*
>   *he is altogether lovely.*
> *This is my lover, this my friend,*
>   *O daughters of Jerusalem.*

Song of Songs 5:10, 16

My husband is the most wonderful man in the world! He is handsome, brilliant, passionate, funny, athletic, wise, and romantic. He is not only a good husband but also my best friend. Sometimes I want to call him in the middle of the day just to talk. I want to tell him everything. My husband knows me better than anyone else, and he sometimes knows why I am upset before I do.

For all his wonderful qualities, my husband is only human. His hair has a funny cowlick, he dislikes doing household or car repairs, he hates talking on the phone, he gets impatient, and he comes dangerously close to forgetting my birthday and our anniversary. Sometimes, no matter how much I want him to be available or to meet my needs, he cannot.

The only one who can ever truly meet all my needs is my Bridegroom, Jesus Christ. He is my husband—my lover and my friend. I must come to Jesus with the same passion and desire, the same friendship and allegiance, with which I approach my human husband. When I need to talk in the middle of the day, I must meet Jesus in prayer. Instead of being critical of my husband when he cannot meet a need, I must look to Jesus, the one who can meet all my needs.

> *The only one who can ever truly meet all my needs is my Bridegroom, Jesus Christ.*

Lord, I praise you that Jesus is my lover and my friend and that he can meet all my needs. Thank you, too, for my human husband, who makes my life so full. Please give me the grace to allow my husband to be human and the strength to trust Jesus to meet all my needs. Amen.

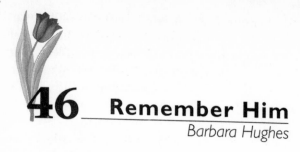

46 Remember Him

Barbara Hughes

My soul is downcast within me;
therefore I will remember you . . .

Psalm 42:6

Sometimes the ministry seems overwhelming. The human dilemma is persistently discouraging. The most disturbing thing for me is when God's people struggle to get along—and even beloved family members have trouble loving each other. At these times, my soul is definitely downcast within me. When I catch myself involuntarily sighing heavy sighs, I know it's time to remember the *therefore* in the verse on which this devotion is based. David is telling us that this is the very time that we *must* remember the Lord.

When I remember my earthly father, I not only think of what he did, I also think of who he was. Remembering the Lord is like that. It's not only remembering answered prayer and God's mighty acts but also remembering him who is my all in all, my creator, my sustainer, my wisdom, my unchanging stalwart, my lover, my just judge, my grace, my guide, my shield, my protector, my goodness, my adequacy, my prince of peace, my Lord and King.

The most disturbing thing for me is when God's people struggle to get along—and even beloved family members have trouble loving each other.

Remembering the Lord lifts my spirit and gives me hope for the future. He has not and will not leave us in our dilemmas. He is able, and his plans will not be thwarted!

Dear Father,

"On my bed I remember you;
    I think of you through the watches
        of the night.
Because you are my help,
    I sing in the shadow of your wings.
My soul clings to you;
    your right hand upholds me" (Psalm 63:6–8).

Amen.

47   **Wind Walker**

Noël Piper

Bless the LORD, O my soul!
O LORD my God, You are very great;
You are clothed with splendor and majesty. . . .
He walks upon the wings of the wind;
He makes the winds His messengers. . . .

Psalm 104:1, 3b–4a NASB

God strolled the beach—
    Our legs and faces blasted by piercing
      sand.
God stepped ashore—
    Palms waved, scattering branches in His
      path.

God strode inland—
    Magnolias, pines, and oaks,
    Who'd stretched one hundred years
      toward God,
    Fell to the ground before Him.

God stood and breathed—
    Our eyes—in dark, closed closet—
Wide opened to His glory.

> *The winds, your*
> *messengers, have opened*
> *our eyes to your greatness.*

Bless the Lord, O my soul! The winds, your messengers, have opened our eyes to your greatness. Praise the Lord! Amen.

48   Make a Wish

Joyce Webster

"What do you want me to do for you?" Jesus asked him. The blind man said, "Rabbi, I want to see." "Go," said Jesus, "your faith has healed you." Immediately he received his sight and followed Jesus along the road.

Mark 10:51–52

Think of being face-to-face with Jesus and hearing him ask, "What do you want me to do for you?" The blind man did not hesitate. He wanted to see.

Magical wishes play a big part in stories, but the blind man wasn't in a "make a wish" situation; he was in the presence of God, where he was given freedom to ask for anything. Jesus not only granted the blind man's request to see, but also gave him a new direction as he followed Jesus. God will meet our request when the answer will compel us to follow him.

One day as I read the entire passage about Jesus' encounter with the blind man, I began to examine my heart. What would *I* have asked from Jesus? This question helped me realize what was valuable to me. I saw clearly where God was leading me and how following him would bring fulfillment to my life.

If there were no limits or no obstacles, for what would you beseech God? We know there are no lim-

What would I have asked from Jesus?

its to his power, compassion, or knowledge. Understanding who God is opens the doors to un-limited possibilities. Write down your wish list. Go over it in the presence of God. Let him add and delete. Give him unrestricted access to your heart. He offers true satisfaction to your soul.

Father, I will not hesitate to speak to you of my desires. You already know every detail of my life and every thought before I think it. As I consider who you are, convince me that allowing you to examine my heart will lead to soul satisfaction. Rabbi, I, too, want to see. Amen.

49 **The Divine Bookkeeper**

Dorothy Kelley Patterson

God is not unjust; he will not forget your work and the love you have shown him as you have helped his people and continue to help them.

Hebrews 6:10

My husband and I were in Jerusalem when we learned that we were being sued. We had accepted the responsibility of caring for a widow. We had maintained her property, including doing repairs and yard work and taking care of her automobile. We employed a student to drive for her and to run errands and even to stay overnight in her home when necessary. She seemed happy and content until an ambitious attorney in the church began to plant seeds of discontent in her heart. He persuaded her to let him sue for her management of her estate. She had never written a check, so she couldn't have managed her estate even if she had wanted to (and she didn't). The matter was quickly settled out of court, with a large amount of money going to the attorney.

It was embarrassing to be sued by someone on whom we had poured our time, energy, creativity, and love—and then to read about it on the front page of the newspaper and also to discover that the

This verse was a good reminder that the Lord takes note of what we do in his name.

perpetrator had identified himself as a believer from our congregation. After our return home, someone gave me a card on which he had written this verse from Hebrews 6: "God is not unjust; he will not forget your work and the love you have shown him as you have helped his people and continue to help them." It was a good reminder that the Lord takes note of what we do in his name, and that this is enough.

Thank you, Lord, for taking note of what I do in your name. What a comforting reminder to know that however unappreciated I may be by those whom I serve, and however unjustly I may be treated—even by fellow believers—you are keeping the books that count. You will not miss anything I say or do in your name, and you will reward me in your time. Amen.

50 Paddle and Pray

Kathy Chapell

I can do everything through [Christ] who gives me strength.

Philippians 4:13

Several years ago we took our children on a canoe trip. I sat in the front of the canoe with our three-year-old daughter, while her brothers and daddy paddled. All went well until we rounded one particularly picturesque bend, and the canoe several hundred yards in front of us disappeared. I mean, it just dropped out of sight. We were headed for a drop in the river channel and some major rapids! Sure enough, the river's current immediately grew fast and rough, the three-year-old began to cry, and my husband shouted from behind me, "Paddle, boys! Paddle!"

"And pray!" I screamed, as I wrapped one arm around my small daughter and gripped the edge of the canoe with the other hand. Down the rapids we flew and over the drop-off into the pool below. Now we were shrieking and laughing, drenched but triumphant. "We did it! Hurrah!" the boys shouted, waving their paddles in the air—and I added, "Thank you, Lord!" at the top of my voice.

This scene often comes to my mind, as we work as hard as we can in our busy lives, coming and going from meeting to soccer game to music lesson to meeting—paddling as fast as we can to get through the rapids and down the river. Paddle, but don't forget to pray. Rejoice in your family and ministry and life—but don't forget to seek the Lord. He gives us the strength to do what he places in our lives. So paddle, and pray.

"Paddle, boys! Paddle! And pray!"

Dear Father, strong and loving, I praise you because I know you are beside me. I know I can call on you and you will hear me. Thank you, Lord. Amen.

51   **Dark Corners**

Jeanne Hendricks

*If one of you should wander from the truth and
someone should bring him back, remember this:
Whoever turns a sinner from the error of his way
will save him from death and cover over a
multitude of sins.*

James 5:19–20

Possibly no dread haunts a mother's heart
more than the specter of a child willfully rejecting
love and sound teaching. Jesus told such a story
when he recounted the family tragedy of the prodigal son (see Luke 15:11–32). The familiar drama,
often replayed in twenty-first-century lives, tracks a
son leaving home with built-in family assets. Soon
he squandered his resources and reduced his life to a
bare subsistence of slavery.

When the prodigal, totally humiliated, came
stumbling back home, the father welcomed him with
open arms and joyful celebration. There's a lesson here
for parents today. Christian families aren't immune to
the heartbreak of a prodigal child, but often we
respond with judgmental disciplines and alienation
rather than with open arms and joyful celebration. All

too often we're like the older brother in Jesus' story who resists accepting the stray back as a full family member. We refuse to ignore the past and to forgive and love again.

The restoration Jesus described requires that we allow God to judge wrongdoing. Our assignment is to foster healing and recovery, to rejoice in regeneration. Finding the lost sheep, the good shepherd joyfully puts it on his shoulders and goes home. The angels in heaven, Jesus said, rejoice over a sinner who repents. Do we?

Christian families aren't immune to the heartbreak of a prodigal child.

As society becomes increasingly menacing for young people, we women must exercise our influence and seek to reclaim the lambs who wander away. As James 5:19–20 reminds us, "Whoever turns a sinner from the error of his way will save him from death and cover over a multitude of sins."

Heavenly Father, grant that I may love the unlovely in my own family and be a godly agent of restoration and renewal. In Jesus' name. Amen.

52 God's Good Work
Sue Sailhamer

And we know that in all things God works for the good of those who love him, who have been called according to his purpose.

Romans 8:28

I'll always remember the day my father died and my world changed forever. He was fifty-seven years old and the hero of my life.

My mother received a phone call that announced that Dad was in cardiac arrest and that she should come to the hospital at once. The forty-five-minute drive seemed to take forever. My uncle was already there and greeted us with the news—"He's gone."

After leading a men's Bible study early that Tuesday morning, Dad had headed off on a long bike ride. He rode about thirty-five miles before suffering a massive heart attack. An off-duty fireman saw his distress and attempted to do CPR. There was comfort in believing that God could have spared him if that were part of his plan.

We found Dad's Bible on his desk, lying open to Philippians 1:21, the passage he had taught to the men that morning: "For to me, to live is Christ and to die is gain." What comfort we derived from knowing that this was my father's final meditation on Scripture!

There was comfort in believing that God could have spared him if that were part of his plan.

Twenty-seven years have passed since that terrible day. I have witnessed God's good work in my life. My wonderful husband, who knew my father, is my new hero. We have two sons who would make their grandpa proud.

God eventually brought my mother a new sweetheart. They were married fifteen years before he, too, went to his eternal home. She is a widow once more, but God is faithful. There is comfort in seeing that we can trust God's promises, even in our darkest moments.

Thank you, Lord, that I can trust you to weave the events of my life into a tapestry of your grace. Help me to trust you, Father, in times of sorrow as well as in times of joy. In Jesus' name. Amen.

53 Looking for Truth
Mary Lou Whitlock

Love suffers long and is kind; love does not envy; love does not parade itself, is not puffed up; does not behave rudely, does not seek its own, is not provoked, thinks no evil; does not rejoice in iniquity, but rejoices in the truth; bears all things, believes all things, hopes all things, endures all things. Love never fails.

1 Corinthians 13:4–8a NKJV

Truth is a rare commodity in our culture. And often those of us who love truth fail to go to the only source of truth for guidance and answers. There it sits on our table or beside our bed—the fountain of truth. We have a long list of needs, crises, and decisions. We fret and fuss about what to do or how to handle our problems. Do we allow God's Word, the book of truth, to infiltrate those arenas. Do we seek a principle, a passage, or even a verse to give us a good and godly response to the situations we face?

We try so hard as wives to solve everything for everyone who lives under our roof. We encourage, console, comfort, plan, plot, and organize in order to make life grand for our family and even for the family of faith. But to get at the truth of how best to go about these things, we often skip along the tip of the wave, walking and talking in generalities we seem to only hope are rooted in Christian doctrine and faith.

Do we seek a principle, a passage, or even a verse to give us a good and godly response to the situations we face?

Today let's stop and ask our questions about the living of our lives to the author of life. Let's seek his truth and wisdom about the people we encounter and decisions we face. How do we touch the lives of our spouses, children, neighbors, church members? Scripture holds the key to all truth in our relationships. Love "rejoices in the truth," as Paul beautifully reminds us in 1 Corinthians 13:6.

Loving heavenly Father, help us today to ponder the depth of your truth for us as we live our lives. Give us strength to live in love in all we do and say. Amen.

54   Imitators

Mary Kassian

> *Be imitators of God, therefore, as dearly loved*
> *children and live a life of love, just as Christ*
> *loved us and gave himself up for us as a fragrant*
> *offering and sacrifice to God.*
>
> *Ephesians 5:1–2*

The tone of voice. The facial expression. The angry words. My young son mimicked me precisely as he chided the dog for its misbehavior. The realization hit me as though God had held up a mirror for me to observe my own behavior, and I didn't like the image that was reflected.

Children pick up the mannerisms of their parents. In John 8:41 Jesus accused the Pharisees of "doing the things your own father does." Their mannerisms and behavior revealed that their father was the devil, not God. Children of God act like God. They imitate him.

Have you ever seen a mime? The pantomime was a popular form of entertainment among ancient Greeks and Romans. An actor or comedian would portray actual persons and events for the audience.

The portrayal required that the actor be extremely adept at the art of imitation in order to reflect the likeness of his subject.

As imitators of God, we copy Christ's behavior and manner in order to reflect his likeness. Because he loves, we love. Because he forgives, we forgive. Because he is kind, we are kind. Because he is humble, we are humble. Because he denies himself for the sake of others, we also deny ourselves for the sake of others.

Imitating Jesus, particularly his love and self-sacrifice, is what dearly loved children do.

Unlike a pantomime, this behavior is not an act; it is part of the process of being transformed into Christ's image. As we imitate him, we become more like him. Imitating Jesus, particularly his love and self-sacrifice, is what dearly loved children do.

Dear Father, help me to be an imitator of your Son, Jesus. I want to learn how to love like he loves, forgive like he forgives, be humble and kind like he is, deny myself like he does, and be holy like he is. Today transform me more into his likeness. Amen.

127

55 God's Favor to Your Husband

Jani Ortlund

*He who finds a wife finds what is good
and receives favor from the LORD.*

Proverbs 18:22

You are God's favor to your husband. It's as though, when God created your husband, he said, "How can I bless this man who is going to serve me all of his life? How can I show him my favor? I know. I'll make_____ [fill in your name] to love him and help him. I'll knit their hearts together. As she follows me, she'll bring him good, not harm. He will develop confidence in her and value her more than any of life's treasures" (see Proverbs 31:10–12).

God has chosen you to live with a man who
is devoted to serving others for the glory of Christ. Your husband needs you. You are the one he turns to for comfort and strength and counsel. He needs your support and participation in his labors. He needs you to "favor" him by understanding and respecting the eternal importance of his work.

How can you be God's favor to your husband?

- Build him up with your words (Ephesians 4:29).
- Watch over the affairs of your household (Proverbs 31:27).
- Leave vengeance to God (Romans 12:19).
- Do what is right, without giving way to your fears (1 Peter 3:6).

God has chosen you to live with a man who is devoted to serving others for the glory of Christ. Your husband needs you.

You are God's favor to your husband. God made you to help meet your husband's physical, intellectual, and spiritual needs. Recommit yourself to embrace your marriage and bring good to your husband all the days of your life.

God, I'm sorry when I've been more of a hindrance than a favor to my husband. Forgive my impatient, independent spirit. Open my heart to new ways to favor this man you have given me. Help me to bring him good, not harm, all the days of my life. In Jesus' name. Amen.

56 The Power of Sincerity

Paulette Washington

I no longer call you servants. . . . Instead, I have called you friends, for everything that I learned from my Father I have made known to you.

John 15:15

Transparency is critical for effectiveness in ministry. The true irony is that everything within us seems to move us away from transparency. After many experiences and interactions, we can conclude that hiding ourselves from others is far safer. And that's true. It *is* safer to hide and to not allow others to see or know us.

Yet the real power of ministry lies in our confidence in God to care for our needs of safety and security. When we commit to be known by others through our intentional decision to be transparent, we pave the way for building trust in relationships. Without that trust, relationships will not grow. That is the rub in all of this. Relationships are built on transparency, and yet this same transparency is what gets us hurt.

This key is the confidence that we have in God. Without that confidence I would never take the kind of risk that is necessary for significant relationships to grow.

Relationships are built on transparency, and yet this same transparency is what gets us hurt.

Take the risk today to be sincere and transparent. There is always the chance that you might get hurt, but what is built in the process is worth it.

Lord, help me to place my trust and security in you alone. And as I embrace you in that confidence, enable me to be transparent and open with others. Amen.

57 Privileged Partners

Mary K. Mohler

See to it that no one misses the grace of God and that no bitter root grows up to cause trouble and defile many.

Hebrews 12:15

Do you sometimes feel as though you are living on a deserted island? Your husband goes off to another meeting—again. Your kids are engrossed in their own activities. Your friendships are shallower than you'd like, perhaps because other women think you are too busy or "too important" to be their friend. Loneliness creeps in and can become as pervasive as kudzu vines.

As ministry wives, many of us can go through phases when we border on envy—even with regard to little things. The grass always seems greener in the layperson's yard. I heard about one ministry wife who filled out a visitors' card requesting a home visit from the pastor—her husband! Those in secular careers just seem to have it made. They can even take vacations without fear of being disturbed by other people's emergencies.

Women, we must step back and remind ourselves what a privilege it is to be a partner in ministry. Yes, there are inconveniences, and yes, we can resent how people demand so much of our husbands and rob us of time with them. But beware of letting these frustrations give way to a root of bitterness. Satan will use it to his full advantage as he attempts to derail you in any way he can. Resolve to make the best of bad situations. Insist on planning flexible family events, as well as regular dates with your husband. The church will respect you for making your family a priority.

Loneliness creeps in and can become as pervasive as kudzu vines.

Bitterness often follows loneliness. Don't let it happen to you.

Lord, may we seek your face as soon as we detect a shred of bitterness. Remind us that you alone can meet all our needs according to your glorious riches in Christ Jesus. Amen.

58   **A Work of Art**

Kathy Hicks

For we are [God's] workmanship, created in Christ Jesus for good works, which God prepared beforehand so that we would walk in them.

Ephesians 2:10 NASB

My husband and I worked at a Christian conference center for twenty years. For many of those years I ran the crafts program. I loved providing the materials and opportunities for people to express themselves creatively, and I enjoyed sharing their pleasure in their creations. It was especially fun when people with real artistic ability would take a simple item, like a plain wooden box, and turn it into a work of art. Everyone who saw what they were doing would stop to admire their workmanship.

134

The word *workmanship* in Ephesians 2:10 implies skill on the part of the person who is doing the work. One dictionary definition is "the quality imparted to a thing in the process of making it." Just as an original painting with the artist's signature has value because of who the artist is, we have value because of who created us. We are *God's* workmanship, and, as the expression goes, "God don't make no junk!"

We aren't just some little craft project, with no real reason for existence. We were created with a particular purpose in mind—"for good works, which God prepared beforehand so that we would walk in them." We are allowed to feel good about his design (see Psalm 139:13–16) and to rejoice in our own unique qualities and gifts. Don't try to be someone else or try to reproduce her ministry. Be the best that God intended you to be, allowing him to do those good works he planned to accomplish through you.

Just as an original painting with the artist's signature has value because of who the artist is, we have value because of who created us.

Wonderful Creator, thank you for your purposeful design of my life. Help me to see myself the way you do. Empower me to do the good works you have planned for me to do. Amen.

59 Going for the Goal

Heather Olford

> *I press on toward the goal to win the prize for which God has called me heavenward in Christ Jesus.*
>
> *Philippians 3:14*

In order to press on toward the goal, we have to forget those things that are behind and reach toward what is ahead (see Philippians 3:13). If there have been times of failure in our lives, they need to be forgiven and forgotten. When the Lord forgives, he forgets. It is hard for us to forget past failures. But we must. We must forget successes, too. If they bring encouragement, it is a blessing, but to dwell on past successes instead of pressing on to do new things for God is to be hindered in our race for the prize.

As women in ministry, and as pastors' wives in particular, we must sense the adventure of knowing that we have a planned pathway to follow. Ephesians 2:10 is such a source of encouragement, as we realize we are "God's workmanship, created in Christ Jesus to do good works, which God prepared in advance for us to do." The goal toward which we must press on is our enjoyment of all that God has prepared for us in Christ Jesus. All that he has planned can be realized by the enabling power of God the Holy Spirit.

The goal toward which we must press on is our enjoyment of all that God has prepared for us in Christ Jesus.

This is an important lesson to heed as we seek to serve our Lord in a world of such busyness that we can be easily distracted from life's real goal, which is ultimately to be like Jesus.

Lord Jesus, you steadfastly set your face to do your Father's will. Enable me, by your Holy Spirit, to do the same. For your dear name's sake. Amen.

60   **Faithfulness**

Lisa Ryken

*He will keep you strong to the end, so that you
will be blameless on the day of our Lord Jesus
Christ. God, who has called you into fellowship
with his Son Jesus Christ our Lord, is faithful.*

1 Corinthians 1:8–9

One of my greatest fears is that in the final
judgment it will be revealed that I have not been
faithful. This thought especially bothered me during
the weeks preceding my husband's installation as the
senior minister of our large-city church. I replayed in
my mind all the times I had failed to be bold in talking about my faith with coworkers and neighbors.
How could I be the wife of a minister in a secular city
and not be confident about my witness as a believer?
What kind of opposition or persecution would we
face? The weight of responsibility and fear of the
future came crushing down on me until I could
scarcely move.

The naked truth is that I *cannot* be faithful. But
God is faithful! God has promised that he will keep me
strong to the end. The only way I can ever be faithful

to God is by grasping hold of the truth that *God is faithful.* God has been faithful to his people down through the centuries, and he has been faithful to me over the short span of my life. God would not have asked me to be faithful to him had he not already committed himself in faithfulness to me. I rest in the words of the psalmist, "Your faithfulness continues through all generations" (Psalm 119:90).

> *God would not have asked me to be faithful to him had he not already committed himself in faithfulness to me.*

Great is your faithfulness, O God, my Father! Please forgive me for being an unfaithful servant. Keep reminding me when I am unfaithful in the little things. Thank you for your promise to be faithful and to keep me strong to the end. May I be found faithful, through the grace of Jesus. Amen.

61   The Mind of Christ

Barbara Hughes

But we have the mind of Christ.

1 Corinthians 2:16b

"Hello, Mrs. Hughes, we were wondering if you might be our speaker for . . ." I am often asked to teach or speak in some capacity because I am the pastor's wife. When I was younger, I jumped at these opportunities, naively thinking I would be good at it because I like public speaking. But over the years I've become far more hesitant and far less confident about accepting these opportunities. Why? First of all, because I've become more conscious of the scriptural warning that "not many of you should presume to be teachers, my brothers, because you know that we who teach will be judged more strictly" (James 3:1). And, second, I know that there are others who are far better equipped and more capable than I am for the task.

But I must be careful not to use this biblically informed hesitance and prideful lack of confidence as an excuse not to do what God has prepared for me to do for the kingdom. Scripture teaches that both our power and wisdom for ministry come from God:

> For the foolishness of God is wiser than man's wisdom, and the weakness of God is stronger than man's strength.
> Brothers, think of what you were when you were called. Not many of you were wise by human standards; not many were influential; not many were of noble birth. But God chose the foolish things of the world to shame the wise; God chose the weak things of the world to shame the strong.
>
> 1 Corinthians 1:25–27

I am often asked to teach or speak in some capacity because I am the pastor's wife.

And then, some twenty verses later, comes the verse on which this devotion is based, which states that God has given those of us who are weak and trembling the very *mind of Christ*, that we might do his work.

May the mind of Christ, my Savior, live in me from day to day, by his love and power controlling all I do and say. (Kate B. Wilkinson) Amen.

62   **Spring Song**
Noël Piper

Sing to the LORD a new song;
   sing to the LORD, all the earth.

Psalm 96:1

The calendar said it was spring, but hard-layered, dirty deposits of snow still covered Minneapolis curbsides, and the sky looked like an old gray sweatshirt.

Before 5:00 on this Sunday morning, my husband had already slipped out of our room and into his study to pray and to prepare himself for the Lord's Day ahead. So, with half the warmth of our bed gone, out of drowsy habit I had curled more snugly under the quilts to sleep a little while longer until the radio alarm would seep into my consciousness and drag me into the dismal day.

Suddenly my eyes flew open at an almost forgotten sound. It had been months! Even through the tightly sealed, double-glazed windows, I heard the song of a bird—not the metallic chirping of a winter sparrow but the real *music* of a robin. Instantly wide-awake, in one movement I threw off the covers and jumped out of bed. I darted from window to window, trying to see the singer. Inside I bubbled like a child on Christmas morning.

> I threw off the covers and jumped out of bed. I darted from window to window, trying to see the singer.

What a gift! God's creation was singing its song, and it filled me up. What did I need with sleep? God made that one small bird so that it would declare his glory.

I went to church later that morning, not out of gray, dull habit, but already worshiping, honoring our great God who uses a creature as small and skittish as a bird to startle us awake to who he is.

O God, all the earth sings to you. You are strong and beautiful and great! Please open my eyes to hear and see more and more of your glory, and then open my mouth to declare it. Amen.

63   **A Better Home**

Joyce Webster

Calling his disciples to him, Jesus said, "I tell you the truth, this poor widow has put more into the treasury than all the others. They all gave out of their wealth; but she, out of her poverty, put in everything—all she had to live on."

Mark 12:43–44

Better Homes and Gardens magazine has never asked to do a feature on our home, and no requests have come for a segment on *Martha Stewart Living* to spotlight the gourmet meals on our table. Nevertheless, our whole family has enjoyed making new friends, cultivating deep relationships, and cherishing precious memories from guests who have stayed in our home. Many of our friends have nicer and bigger homes than we do, but we still place great value on using everything God has given us in carrying out a ministry to others.

We would have missed out on so much if we had allowed the deficiencies of our house to dictate the use of our home. When 1 Peter 4:9 directs us to "offer hospitality to one another without grumbling," there is an acknowledgment that being hos-

144

pitable may give way to grumbling about everything from lack of amenities to the frequency of guests. Yet the reality is we have an opportunity to give to God's treasury as well. It is an eternal investment. The poor widow woman gave out of her poverty. My devotion and my commitment to God are solely dependent on who God is and not on what I have to offer. He will use whatever I surrender to him.

> Many of our friends have nicer and bigger homes than we do, but we still place great value on using everything God has given us in carrying out a ministry to others.

Father, give me your perspective on my offerings. Keep me from focusing on limitations. Help me use everything I have in order to make eternal investments in your kingdom. Assure me that you honor my heart above my gifts. Amen.

64

She Did What She Could

Dorothy Kelley Patterson

"She did what she could. She poured perfume on my body beforehand to prepare for my burial."

Mark 14:8

While in seminary, my husband and I took into our home a teenage girl whose mother had abused her. No one else wanted to get involved. We were touched by her need and asked the court to place her in our custody. However, in less than a decade she pulled away from our loving discipleship. One Sunday morning, while we were at church, she took her clothes and furnishings from her room and left. Other than an occasional appearance, she never returned to our family circle.

Never have I experienced any greater devastation, nor have I experienced any more complete failure. I grieved for months. I went through each day staggering under a heavy burden. I wanted to correct the mistakes and find a solution to this problem. I wanted a spiritual victory. Even today I don't know where our adopted daughter lives. I have no knowledge of what my two grandsons are doing. Burdens like this sap your strength and leave a shadow of darkness across your life.

Burdens like this sap your strength and leave a shadow of darkness across your life.

A woman broke an alabaster jar of expensive perfume and poured it over the head of Jesus. Some criticized her for wasting what could have been sold to provide money for ministry. But Jesus knew that she was honoring him. His words in Mark 14:8 are precious to me as well—*She did what she could.*

Lord, I do rejoice that I am your child. I am grateful for the opportunities to invest in lives and to nurture the next generation. I am grateful that I don't face life's challenges alone. I must simply be willing to do what I can with what I have while I can where I can—and then leave the results to you. Amen.

65

We Just
Can't Fix It

Kathy Chapell

*Now is your time of grief, but I will see you again
and you will rejoice, and no one will take away
your joy.*

John 16:22

Our good friend Joanie was bright, pretty, and fun—and she loved the Lord dearly. One night as she drove home from choir practice, a drunk driver hit her car head-on, and Joanie was killed. The whole church was wracked with grief, and Joanie's parents were overwhelmed by the death of this cherished daughter.

As a young pastor's wife, untouched by any personal experience with loss, I had no idea what to say. I wanted to help—to say something that would bring comfort, something that would make it better. All I could do was sit with Joanie's parents and cry.

One night, shortly after the accident, I tried to express to my husband, not only my own grief at Joanie's death, but also my frustration at not being able to help her mother. My wise husband put his arms around me and said, "Sweetheart, sometimes you just can't fix it."

Sometimes we just can't fix the hurts in this world and in our churches. The truth is that only Christ can ease the pain, and he must do it in his time. In the meantime, we can only comfort others with our love and presence and tears, as we trust our Father to work his perfect healing.

All I could do was sit with Joanie's parents and cry.

O Father, help me to know that you are the God of all comfort. Give me tears to share with my brothers and sisters and a heart that yearns to find solace in you. Amen.

149

66   I'm Afraid

Jeanne Hendricks

All those gathered here will know that it is not by sword or spear that the LORD saves; for the battle is the LORD's....

1 Samuel 17:47

As a young child I often visited my Aunt Emma during my summer vacations. Terrified of thunderstorms, she would disappear into her large pantry at the first distant clap of thunder. She said she couldn't bear to see the lightning. Conversely, I took great delight in sitting as close as possible to the window as the rain cascaded down, so that I could catch a glimpse of the brilliant flashes of lightning and then shiver when the thunder crashed. I loved watching the trees blow in the wind and the rivulets of water race past the front gate.

Why does one event make one person fearful and another energized? The book of 1 Samuel describes a battle scene where the invincible Philistines had deployed their attack forces, headed by a giant named Goliath. The Israelites were paralyzed with fear, but young David, who had come on the scene with food rations, viewed Goliath differently.

"Who is this uncircumcised Philistine that he should defy the armies of the living God?" David inquired (1 Samuel 17:26), and then he volunteered to meet the enemy one-on-one. We all know the story of how David chose five smooth stones from a stream and with his sharp-shooting slingshot managed to fell the enemy with a missile to the head.

Any human fear can be turned into a beatable opponent when we view it through God's eyes.

It is not by sword or spear that the LORD saves; for the battle is the LORD's. With those triumphant words David not only inspired the fearful army of God's people but also revealed his own focus of faith—and the key to defeating fear. Just as we can view thunderstorms as a display of God's creative power, any human fear can be turned into a beatable opponent when we view it through God's eyes.

Heavenly Father, take my fears and sift them through your power. Disarm them, so that I will trust in you and not be afraid. In Jesus' name. Amen.

67 The End from the Beginning

Sue Sailhamer

> *I wait for the LORD, my soul waits,*
> *and in his word I put my hope.*

Psalm 130:5

I was newly pregnant with our second son the night my husband came home from an elders board meeting and told me he had resigned as associate pastor. I was stunned. He seemed just as surprised.

I knew he'd had philosophical differences with the senior pastor, and that my husband's days at the church were very likely numbered, but what transpired at the board meeting that November evening convinced him to resign on the spot.

In one sense it was a huge relief to be free from the burden of ministering where we no longer felt we fit. The wounds, however, were deep. My husband had been at the church for fourteen years, nine of them before we were married.

What about our future? How would we survive financially? What would we do? There were a hundred questions—and no answers. Our only option was to trust God.

In the days that followed, the Lord provided for our financial needs. He opened doors that led us to a new place of ministry. I'll admit I was skeptical at first, assuming that all churches were alike. We began ministry at a place where neither of us knew anyone.

It was a huge relief to be free from the burden of ministering where we no longer felt we fit.

As I look back on that time in our lives, I am truly thankful for those difficult days twenty-one years ago. God turned our pain and disappointment into blessing. He led us to a place of healing and to a new ministry home where we spent the next nineteen years.

When you are misunderstood, be assured that God understands. Wait on him. He knows the end from the beginning. Trust his faithfulness!

Lord, my hope is not in my circumstances; my hope is in you and in your Word. Help me to look to your promises as I wait on you. Amen.

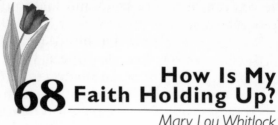

68 How Is My Faith Holding Up?

Mary Lou Whitlock

Come to me, all you who are weary and burdened, and I will give you rest.

Matthew 11:28

If someone tugged at that loose piece of yarn in your life, would your world start to unravel? Life is complex. Activities seem to continually increase, and demands from family and ministry never subside. Satan uses these circumstances to make small dents in our armors of faith, and we ask, "Lord, is it worth the sacrifice?" We mutter that we have no time to ourselves and that no one appreciates us. "What about all those promises, Lord?" We are daughters of the King, but we feel more like paupers who just drift along aimlessly.

Look again with fresh eyes at the invitation Jesus extends in the verse on which this devotion is based: "Come to me, all you who are weary and burdened, and I will give you rest." Do you need this rest today, this gentle peace? Do you need a place of solace where you can turn your heart and soul to the Lord of peace? As a sinner saved by grace, go to the Lord and let his peace flow over you. He is near. He is a fortress and a shelter from the storms of life.

We are daughters of the King, but we feel more like paupers who just drift along aimlessly.

No burden was heavier than the one our Lord carried that night long ago in the Garden of Gethsemane. He bore every real and conceivable burden we could mention. Will we trust him today to help us with our cares, our anxieties (real and imagined), and our fears? He has promised never to leave or forsake us. Nothing can separate us from the love of God. Sisters, immerse yourselves in these truths today.

Heavenly Father, we don't know why our burdens seem so large to us when we recall how much you suffered for our sakes. Help us to release our cares to you and to trust you fully. Give us confidence in your peace and promises, and give us strength and patience to wait on your leading. Amen.

69   **Chain Reaction**

Mary Kassian

We also rejoice in our sufferings, because we know that suffering produces perseverance; perseverance, character; and character, hope. And hope does not disappoint us.

Romans 5:3–5a

My children used to build domino chains on the kitchen floor. They'd knock down that first domino and set off the chain reaction until the last one collapsed. In the verses on which this devotion is based, Paul describes a chain reaction that's put into motion when we respond to trials in the right way. The chain begins with suffering but ends with hope.

Suffering (or *tribulations,* in some Bible trans- 156 lations) is translated from the Greek word *thlipsis,* which means "pressing, pressure." The term was used of squeezing olives in a press to extract the oil or squeezing grapes to extract the juice. When we are "squeezed" by suffering, the Lord extracts perseverance from us.

Perseverance is a spiritual fortitude that bears up under, and is made even stronger by, suffering. It's the marathon runner's resolve to keep running to the end. Perseverance leads to character. The Greek term denotes character of a "proven" nature—like precious metals that have been tested and found pure. This leads in the end to a deeper hope in the glory of God.

When we are "squeezed" by suffering, the Lord extracts perseverance from us.

It is in suffering that we exercise hope by persevering and by being tested and proved pure in the middle of seemingly hopeless circumstances. This process results in an even deeper conviction of the reality and certainty of that for which we hope (see Romans 4:18–19).

When we feel the pain of that first domino's fall, we can be confident that when the last one falls, Jesus Christ will have produced in us a deeper certainty in his goodness and love and in our destiny as children of God.

Dear Father, thank you that at the end of suffering I will have a deeper hope and certainty in you. Thank you for using difficult circumstances to increase my perseverance, character, and hope. Amen.

70 Kindness in the Face of Criticism

Jani Ortlund

> *We work hard with our own hands. When we are cursed, we bless; when we are persecuted, we endure it; when we are slandered, we answer kindly.*
>
> *1 Corinthians 4:12–13a*

Full-time ministry is just plain hard work. It's late-night phone calls and early-morning meetings. It's working weekends and holidays. It calls for a deep and oftentimes painful involvement with your flock. It requires compelling ways to present the gospel. It is not, as someone once quipped to me, "a job that allows you a weeklong quiet time."

As we work hard, Jesus calls us to bless those who curse us and pray for those who persecute us (see Luke 6:28; Matthew 5:44). Persecutions can take the form of people who persistently annoy you, church members who make life difficult for your family. God calls us to endure persecution without yielding to grumbling, gossip, or revenge.

Christian leaders will be maligned and belittled, even vilified. If certain persons treated Jesus with contempt during his time on earth, why should we be exempt? Not only are we to endure these difficulties patiently, we are to be profoundly kind in the midst of them.

Persecutions can take the form of people who persistently annoy you, church members who make life difficult for your family.

When people misrepresent your husband's motives, words, and mannerisms and when they gossip about his family, budget, car, and hobbies, you are to answer kindly. You are to be tender, generous, and gracious. As the apostle Paul reminds us, God will honor you with his praise when "those who have been given a trust [have been proved] faithful. . . . [God] will bring to light what is hidden in darkness and will expose the motives of men's hearts. At that time each will receive his praise from God" (1 Corinthians 4:2, 5).

O Father, I am so prickly. Just a whiff of criticism, and I lash out—if not verbally, then in my heart. I know it's wrong to do so, and I'm sorry. Forgive me. Bless those who curse me and persecute me. Help me to speak peace to them. Forgive me my debts, as I forgive my debtors. In the name of your tenderhearted Son, Jesus. Amen.

71   Growing in Sensitivity

Paulette Washington

Instead, speaking the truth in love, we will in all things grow up into him who is the Head, that is, Christ.

Ephesians 4:15

The basic definition of sensitivity is "the gaining of knowledge about another person in order to relate empathetically with her." The challenge for anyone in ministry, particularly women in ministry with their husbands, is to grow in sensitivity. It is not too difficult to develop this sensitivity for those we love and care about. The real challenge comes in developing this sensitivity for those who have harmed us—or our husbands.

Early in our ministry at Rock Church I came to realize that I had deeply wounded a number of women in our church. It was the result of my insensitivity to what they were going through, as well as my unwillingness to give enough of myself so that I could gain knowledge about them and begin to understand them better. The outcome was considerable misunderstanding and miscommunication.

Because I had been careful not to share a lot of myself, the problems had been compounded. Sensitivity is a two-way street where each person is committed to gaining the necessary knowledge about the other in order to see the world through her eyes. So practicing sensitivity also includes sharing something of ourselves when the other person is seeking to gain knowledge about us.

> *The real challenge comes in developing this sensitivity for those who have harmed us— or our husbands.*

I have come to conclude that the three most powerful words I can say to another person are "help me understand." These words reflect a *commitment* to wanting to know the other person deeply enough to ask and listen to their response.

Evaluate your relationships. Where would you rate on the sensitivity scale with those significant persons in your life? If you fall short of where you think you should be, take steps to ask "help me understand" the next time you're together.

God, help me to practice sensitivity in all my relationships. Open my eyes and heart to the needs of others, and help me to minister to them in your name. Amen.

72   **No Substitute**

Mary K. Mohler

Yet the news about him spread all the more, so that crowds of people came to hear him and to be healed of their sicknesses. But Jesus often withdrew to lonely places and prayed.

Luke 5:15–16

Is your to-do list for today replete with ministry-related activities? Think back for a moment to Jesus' ministry. Consider that literally thousands of people longed for the touch of his healing hand. Yet did he spend all day and night healing the masses, especially knowing that his days on earth were fleeting? No. Scripture plainly states that Jesus often withdrew for time alone with the Father. How much more do we need to carefully guard our activities to ensure we have time alone with our Lord!

Teaching a women's Bible study is commendable, but it is not time alone with God. Praying with a friend as she lies in a hospital bed is admirable, but it is not time alone with God. Preparing a meal for a family in crisis is indeed biblical, but it is not time alone with God.

I speak from experience. It's easy to justify these wonderful acts of service. We give and give sacrificially to others. Praise God. But we must never think that these acts serve as a substitute for time spent daily seeking God's face through prayer, Bible study, and simple quietness as we listen for that still, small voice. Dear sister, we must model for our children and for the women we are privileged to influence how paramount our time with the Lord is. Jesus led by example. Follow him!

How much more do we need to carefully guard our activities to ensure we have time alone with our Lord!

Father, give us every day the discipline to seek your face in the most personal way. Convict us when we try to use ministry activities as a substitute for personal piety. Don't let us rest until we have heard a word from you today. In Jesus' name. Amen.

73 Clueless in Prayer

Kathy Hicks

Do not be anxious about anything, but in everything, by prayer and petition, with thanksgiving, present your requests to God. And the peace of God, which transcends all understanding, will guard your hearts and your minds in Christ Jesus.

Philippians 4:6–7

We all face situations in which we either have no clue what to do, or we don't have the ability or resources to solve it. When I find myself in these situations, I've discovered a little course of action that helps me give it up to God's responsibility—which is where it belongs. This exercise relieves me of the anxiety I experience when I feel the need to fix the problem myself.

I remember a time when my daughter was very upset about something. I couldn't solve it for her and didn't have a clue how to comfort her. As I prayed for her, I remember stretching out my hands as though holding an invisible box that contained her problem. As I lifted it up to the Lord, I prayed, *I don't know what to do with this, Lord. I need you to take it and solve it for me. I can't do it.* It was amazing how the simple physical action of handing over that problem to the Lord helped bring peace to my heart. This physical action represented my dependence on God and my submission to his will in this situation. Since that time it's become my way of expressing my trust in him and reminding myself that these problems are no longer mine to worry about. He is my problem solver.

> It was amazing how the simple physical action of handing over that problem to the Lord helped bring peace to my heart.

All-powerful Father, thank you for being bigger than any problem I could ever have. Thank you for the peace that comes from knowing that you have the power and the desire to care for me as your beloved daughter. Help me to go to you and ask rather than to worry. Amen.

74   **Dying to Live**

Heather Olford

Unless a grain of wheat falls into the ground and dies, it remains alone; but if it dies, it produces much grain.

John 12:24 NKJV

    Dying to live is an essential principle in our Christian experience. Two lines from an old hymn remind us: "Dying with Jesus, by death reckoned mine, living with Jesus a new life divine" (Daniel W. Whittle).

    This was the truth Jesus shared with his followers. In order to live we must die like the "grain of wheat," and when we die, "we produce much grain." Paul says the same thing when he tells us to count ourselves dead to sin but alive to God in Christ Jesus (see Romans 6:11).

    As we rely on the Holy Spirit to make this real in us day by day (see Romans 8:13), we come alive. As my husband, Stephen, often states, we should accept every attack on our self life as "the nails of the Cross" in order to be freed from lusts, jealousies, bitterness, and wrong ambitions. As the misdeeds of the body are put to death, the resurrection life of Jesus comes through our personalities, and the fruit of the Spirit is revealed (see Galatians 5:22–24).

We should accept every attack on our self life as "the nails of the Cross."

As pastors' wives, we need to know this conformity to Christ's death if we are going to demonstrate the life of Jesus Christ to others. If the grain of wheat does not die, it remains alone; there will be no golden harvest. But if it dies, "it produces much grain." Remember the words of Jesus: "He who hates his life in this world will keep it for eternal life" (John 12:25 NKJV)

Oh, to be saved from myself, dear Lord,
Oh, to be lost in Thee;
Oh, that it may be no more I,
But Christ that lives in me!
(Mrs. A. A. Whiddington)
Amen.

75   My Home Place

Lisa Ryken

*One thing I ask of the L*ORD*,*
  this is what I seek:
*that I may dwell in the house of the L*ORD
  all the days of my life,
*to gaze upon the beauty of the L*ORD
  and to seek him in his temple.

Psalm 27:4

I grew up in a Christian home and was taken to church from the days of my infancy, but my family rarely went to the evening worship service. My husband's family, on the other hand, went to the evening service every week. After we got married I had a job as a schoolteacher and wanted Sunday evenings to prepare for an early start on Monday morning. For several years we had a running conflict about evening church attendance.

Actually, the problem was not about church attendance as much as it was about my attitude. I resented the time it took to attend church. I did not beg God that I could live in his house and gaze upon his beauty. So when God called us to a church where my husband's primary job was to preach at the evening service, I had to laugh. As I began to worship and hear God's Word regularly on Sunday evenings,

The problem was not about church attendance as much as it was about my attitude.

I was convicted of my sinful attitude. I began to desire to gaze upon God's beauty in those evening services. My desire was further fueled by listening to Michael Card's *Psalm 23*, which translates the phrase in verse 6 "dwell in the house of the LORD" as "make my home place in the house of the LORD." As a homemaker this resonated with me. God's house is a place of comfort, healing, and security. It is a place where I can take my shoes off and be at rest. More and more my desire is to spend all the days of my life in God's house.

Lord, I praise you that you are beautiful. Forgive me for resenting the time given to worship. Give me the desire to seek you in your temple and gaze upon your beauty. Amen.

76   Words of Life

Barbara Hughes

From this time many of his disciples turned back and no longer followed him. "You do not want to leave too, do you?" Jesus asked the Twelve. Simon Peter answered him, "Lord, to whom shall we go? You have the words of eternal life."

John 6:66–68

Christianity has always been radical. In the passage preceding John 6:66–68, we find the religious rulers arguing about Jesus' claim to be the sole bread of life. In fact, many of Jesus' own disciples found his teaching so difficult to accept that they jumped ship. Things haven't changed in our day. Jesus' words still stir up sharp controversy. But now it's *my husband* who is declaring the challenging words of Christ. To be married to a man who dares to proclaim "thus saith the Lord" assuredly means that your life will not be conflict-free. For Jesus' words convict of sin, expose hypocrisy, and cry out against injustice, and they are doggedly countercultural.

Whenever I am tempted to jump ship amidst the inevitable turmoil of following Jesus, his haunting question comes to mind: "You do not want to leave too, do you?" And how I thank God for Simon Peter's faithful response, "Lord, to whom shall we go? You have the words of eternal life."

Jesus' words still stir up sharp controversy.

Dear Father in heaven, thank you for the words of life my husband has been called to preach. May these words of hope and truth so fill my mind that there's no room for fear. Make me a woman of strength and courage, sustained by your Word and unrelenting in gratitude for Jesus and his words of eternal life. Amen.

77   Everyday Help

Noël Piper

Now may our Lord Jesus Christ Himself and God our Father, who has loved us and given us eternal comfort and good hope by grace, comfort and strengthen your hearts in every good work and word.

2 Thessalonians 2:16–17 NASB

It might be my earliest memory. I was standing by the open silverware drawer of the white, ripple-red-edged, metal kitchen table, watching Mother.

"Does Jesus help us do *everything?*" I asked.

"Yes," she replied, "everything." In my three-year-old mind, Jesus took Mother's place at our green-and-cream gas stove. In his white storybook-picture robe, Jesus stood and stirred our supper soup.

I remember almost nothing from the early years of my life. Why, then, is this image fastened so firmly in my mental album? Perhaps because it's true. Not the robes, no. Not the visible Jesus. But what Mother taught me as a child is what I still need to remember. I am dependent on Jesus for every single good work and word, no exceptions—when I'm stirring the stew and setting the silverware, and in every other mundane moment of my day.

Sometimes it's easier to remember that "God is our refuge and strength, an ever-present help in *trouble*" (Psalm 46:1, emphasis added). I *know* I need God when I'm in a crisis. But do I need his strength, his help, any less when I'm answering the phone, running out to get a gallon of milk, wiping a drippy nose, or letting the dog out? No, of course not.

"Does Jesus help us do everything?"

It is Jesus, not we ourselves, who comforts and strengthens our hearts in *every* good work and word—not just in emergencies.

Lord, keep us aware of our total dependence on you. Thank you for your help and strength for every little thing we do and say, all day long, every day. Amen.

78 Looking to Christ

Joyce Webster

My eyes are ever on the LORD,
*   for only he will release my feet from the snare.*
                                          Psalm 25:15

The young mother was well loved and well respected. No one could have imagined that she would be murdered in her home and that her husband, a church leader, would be charged and eventually convicted of the crime. It was a time of sorrow that was filled with more questions than answers. Shock, denial, deep disappointment, and disillusionment settled in.

For most of the people in the church it was a time to draw nearer to God and draw on his power and comfort. For some it was just the opposite. They began to pull away from God and the church. They were disillusioned because a man they had considered to be spiritually strong had failed so tragically. When a Christian leader fails in any way, there are always those who will turn from

God and discount God's ability to work in their own life. If "Mr. or Mrs. Spiritual Giant" can't stay faithful to God, then how could they ever be expected to stay faithful?—so the reasoning goes.

When a Christian leader fails in any way, there are always those who will turn from God and discount God's ability to work in their own life.

We should desire to live in a way that others will want to emulate. Yet the only true model for living is Jesus Christ. When we keep our eyes on God, we are never disillusioned. He fulfills all his promises and purposes.

Lord, protect me from putting anyone above you. I am thankful for those who have led me spiritually and who have set an example of faith. Empower them to lead and give me grace to forgive when they fail. Protect me from turning my gaze from you. I praise you, Lord, that you never disappoint. Amen.

79 The Time-Out Chair

Dorothy Kelley Patterson

> *Do not make light of the Lord's discipline*
> *and do not lose heart when he rebukes you,*
> *because the Lord disciplines those he loves. . . .*
>
> Hebrews 12:5b–6a

My sister-in-law and I found a child's chair that was the exact shade of my blue bedroom walls. The chair had hand-painted butterflies and other creatures and inscribed on it were these words: "Time-Out Chair—Quit Bugging Me!" I simply had to have it. Of course, I didn't know how I would use the chair, since my grandchildren are perfect and never need a time-out chair. I have heard my granddaughter Abigail talk about some nursery school classmates who've had a time-out, and she has suggested that her younger sister Rebekah might need a time-out. In any case, the chair was the right color, and its innovative design made the piece worthy of purchase.

How often has the heavenly Father assigned me to a time-out chair? I rush through day after day, week after week, and even year after year without time to enjoy the process. I want everything to follow the plans I've made and the dreams I've envisioned. Any hitch along the way is resented. On the other hand, the Lord says that the way up is down. You sit down and wait on him in order to go up higher in your relationship with him. So have a "time-out" today.

"Time-Out Chair—

Quit Bugging Me!"

Heavenly Father, let me hurry up and wait. Make my heart quiet and my body still before your throne. Let me take "time-out" myself before you decide to place me in the time-out chair. Let me be still and wait for you to direct me to the next thing. Amen.

80

Let's Look at
the Tigers

Kathy Chapell

But God demonstrates his own love for us in this:
While we were still sinners, Christ died for us.

Romans 5:8

When they were younger our children loved going to the St. Louis Zoo. One particular visit is marked in my mind as "the day the boys almost got eaten by a lion."

The kids and I were having a zoo day with another mom and her three children. We were headed for Big Cat Country—a two-acre habitat designed to give the tigers and lions room to roam while we humans observed them from the bridges above. As the other mom and I strolled our babies up the ramp, the older children romped on ahead of us. When I reached the top of the bridge, I saw my sons—my darlings—on top of a pile of fake boulders overhanging the lions' yard. The boys had squeezed through a gap in the fencing. As they stretched out over the edge, looking for lions, my heart stopped.

All I could think of was that they were going to fall over the edge and be eaten by lions.

My thoughts raced. As much as I wanted to scream at them, I knew that to do so might startle them and cause them to lose their balance. So I forced myself to walk quietly toward the boulders, hold out my arms, and say in the calmest possible tone, "Come, boys. Come get a hug, and we'll go look for the tigers." They obeyed, and they were safe in my arms.

All I could think of was that they were going to fall over the edge and be eaten by lions.

Jesus did that for us, you know. We were on the precipice, in mortal danger, and he held out his arms and spoke to us in love. He stretched out his arms on the cross, calling us to find life in his arms of everlasting love. Now we are safe.

Dear, dear Father, thank you for saving me. Thank you for holding out your loving arms and gathering me back from death. Amen.

81 Best Friend
Jeanne Hendricks

When you pass through the waters,
*   I will be with you;*
and when you pass through the rivers,
*   they will not sweep over you.*
When you walk through the fire,
*   you will not be burned;*
*   the flames will not set you ablaze.*

Isaiah 43:2

We had been good friends since college days. Our husbands were close colleagues, and now I sat beside her bed and asked her what it was like to be dying. Her melanoma had come and gone and come again. She said she didn't feel as though she were dying. I remarked out loud that when we pass through the rivers and the fire, God promises protection. Maybe he would miraculously heal her. But no, I would later kiss her comatose head just before she took her last breath.

It was a worshipful memorial service, recounting the legacy she had left for us. My friend was safely with her Savior. But what about me? The climb would be steeper without my prayer partner; the path would be rougher without her funny comments. I could no longer call and ask her for her wise opinions. Then, as I struggled in my self-pity, I remembered that the promise I had quoted for her was also for me. When I wade through the difficult parental waters alone or shrink from the heat of the fires of ministry misunderstandings, God will not allow me to be overcome by the flood or to be burned.

With every subtraction God multiples himself for the receptive believer.

Human losses in life grow more intense as years pass. But at the same time God's gifts grow more meaningful. With practice, the mature anxious heart finds itself increasingly calmed by God's peace. God's Spirit guides and teaches more clearly the one who learns over the years to listen to him. With every subtraction God multiples himself for the receptive believer.

Dear Father, help me take from your hand whatever you give, knowing that it comes through the screen of your incomparable love. Amen.

82 The Whole Picture
Sue Sailhamer

Finally, all of you, live in harmony with one another; be sympathetic, love as brothers, be compassionate and humble. Do not repay evil with evil or insult with insult, but with blessing, because to this you were called so that you may inherit a blessing.

1 Peter 3:8–9

After the women's Christmas brunch at our church, a woman came up to me and said, "I just wanted to tell you that I forgive you." Her remark caught me by surprise. I didn't know what to say, plus I wasn't even sure I knew who she was. Fortunately, her subsequent comments gave me enough clues to figure out her name. It was Pauline, who had married a widower in the church a few years earlier.

It was obvious that Pauline had mustered up all her courage to explain that she felt my husband and I had slighted her. She somehow believed we purposely ignored her. According to her, my husband would look right past her to greet her husband—and not her.

When I told my husband about the conversation, he was surprised. Perhaps there had been a time or two when he couldn't recall her name—and she took offense at this.

This episode underscored for me a simple reality of ministry: People want a personal connection with you and your family. As a ministry wife there will be times when you're confronted by somebody's unrealistic expectations or hurt feelings. It's inescapable. But there is another side to these encounters. It's all the times church members share encouraging comments and such blessings as homemade jam, box-seat tickets at a sports event, theater tickets, or invitations to a meal in their homes.

> *People want a personal connection with you and your family.*

I've learned to not take a puzzling comment personally but instead to focus on the whole picture. And it surely is worth it to work at remembering people's names!

What a privilege it is, Lord, to serve you by ministering to others. Give me a heart of compassion and humility. Make me a blessing to others as you allow them to bless me. Amen.

83 Children of Light

Mary Lou Whitlock

> *Do not let any unwholesome talk come out of your mouths, but only what is helpful for building others up according to their needs, that it may benefit those who listen.*
>
> *Ephesians 4:29*

A section heading in my Bible reads like this: "Living as Children of Light." It's not easy to submit my life to the teachings of the passage that begins at Ephesians 4:17. Paul is instructing us that if we love the Lord, we must put on the new self—casting off the old self with its deceitful desires. We must speak truthfully and not sin in our anger. And, of course, we must not steal but work faithfully in order to have enough to share with others.

Now comes the really hard part. "Do not let any unwholesome talk come out of your mouths, but only what is helpful for building others up according to their needs, that it may benefit those who listen." I have often thought about the phrase "that it may benefit those who listen." Who does listen to what we say? A wonderful cartoon hit the nail right on the head as it pictured Mom and Dad opening the door to greet a visitor. Their child approaches them, sees the visitor, and remarks loudly, "I don't see a foot in his mouth!" Yes, more people than we think hear our words. We know words have power.

> We know words have power. They can hurt or heal, confuse and complicate or make plain, bring discord and disunity or peace, curse or bless.

They can hurt or heal, confuse and complicate or make plain, bring discord and disunity or peace, curse or bless.

Paul understood this. We cannot make our words *good* words unless we rid ourselves of bitterness, rage and anger, as well as brawling and slander. After that, there is the possibility of being "kind and compassionate to one another, forgiving each other, just as in Christ God forgave you" (Ephesians 4:32). The goal is there for us—to become children of light in the way we use our words. Solomon puts it well, "A word aptly spoken is like apples of gold in settings of silver" (Proverbs 25:11).

Heavenly Father, help me as I speak today to weigh my words, that they might be words of light—your light. Through the power of your Holy Spirit, take away any bitterness or anger. Help me, in the words I speak and in my demeanor, to love others by the way I speak and live. Amen.

84

It Doesn't Disappoint

Mary Kassian

And we rejoice in the hope of the glory of God. . . .
And hope does not disappoint us, because God
has poured out his love into our hearts by the
Holy Spirit, whom he has given us.

Romans 5:2, 5

The quiet voice on the phone was expressionless, emptied of life. My friend was emotionally spent. She was faced with a debilitating illness, a suicidal son, a daughter with learning problems, and a husband on the verge of a breakdown because of his failing business. Medication couldn't stop her spiral into the pit of depression.

Her story is altogether familiar. Almost daily I am confronted with the harsh reality of women who suffer. I often don't know what to say. I can only trust in the promise of Scripture that "hope does not disappoint."

To hope is to desire with *expectation*. It means to long for something with the *certainty* that the desire will be attained. According to Paul, the key to facing suffering is to hope in the right thing—to place our hope in that which is certain. When we face difficult situations, we tend to place our hope in God answering our prayers *our* way. Our hope is that God will follow our agenda. Unfortunately, we are often blind to his plan—and subsequently often disappointed.

> *Almost daily I am confronted with the harsh reality of women who suffer.*

Hope that is certain is not hope for resolution (though we will cry out for our pain and suffering to end), but hope in the glory of God. This glory is the state of Godlikeness that has been lost because of sin but will be restored when we see him face-to-face. Even in the midst of great pain, we can look forward with great anticipation to sharing in the glory of all that God is and all that he has for us. We can cling to the certainty that, in the end, our heavenly Father will make it right.

Dear Father, help me fix my hope firmly on your glory. May your deep love for me fill me with certainty of the future I have in you. Help me remember that you are faithful and true and that I will *not* be disappointed when I put my hope in you. Amen.

85   The Lion House

Jani Ortlund

Be self-controlled and alert. Your enemy the devil prowls around like a roaring lion looking for someone to devour.

1 Peter 5:8

We could hear the lion roaring long before we entered the lion house. Our children rushed ahead of Ray and me to see if that thunderous roar was really coming from a lion. When we caught up with the kids, their eyes were open wide and their hands were covering their ears. On the way home we talked about how glad we were for those iron bars between us and the lions!

The Bible compares Satan to a roaring lion looking for those he can destroy. His malice is directed against God and God's people. We should take our powerful enemy as seriously as we would a ravenous lion.

But remember that, while Satan is superhuman, he is not on God's level. Do not allow him to terrorize you. Christ has triumphed over him, and so will you (see 1 John 4:4). Just as those iron bars protected us from the lions at the zoo, Jesus is your protector who stands between you and Satan, making you "strong, firm and steadfast" (1 Peter 5:10). And one day Satan will be completely silenced (see Revelation 20:10).

Until then, we walk through life as though in a jungle where a hungry lion prowls and roars. Through it all Peter calls us to remain alert. So we encourage each other to be watchful and levelheaded and to find our strength "in the Lord and in his mighty power . . . so that you can take your stand against the devil's schemes" (Ephesians 6:10–11).

Satan is a real enemy, but he is doomed. Christ will muzzle the beast.

Satan is a real enemy, but he is doomed. Christ will muzzle the beast.

Dear Father, thank you for not letting Satan devour me in my weakness. Make me strong, firm, and steadfast by the blood of your precious Son, who will overcome the accuser of our sisters and brothers. In Jesus' name. Amen.

86

Acceptance Speech

Kathy Hicks

> *May the God who gives endurance and encouragement give you a spirit of unity among yourselves as you follow Christ Jesus, so that with one heart and mouth you may glorify the God and Father of our Lord Jesus Christ.*
>
> *Accept one another, then, just as Christ accepted you, in order to bring praise to God.*
>
> Romans 15:5–7

To my shame I have to admit that some people are just hard for me to be around. I find some people to be less "acceptable" than others—whether it is a difference in lifestyle, background, values, or social graces. It's easier to avoid them than spend time with them.

Not long ago I was doing some behind-the-scenes preparation for an event, and someone told me that "Chris" might be available to help me. I secretly hoped Chris wouldn't show up. She was one of those people I found difficult to put up with. Besides some social quirks, which I didn't understand but assumed were the result of something lacking in Chris's background, she also had what I considered to be an unseemly over-respect for my position of leadership—something that always makes me feel uncomfortable.

Chris came, but she was in a bad mood—something I hadn't experienced in any of our previous encounters. Ironically, her negative mood moved the conversation in a way that would surprise me. We experienced a level of communication and acceptance over the next couple of hours that amazed both of us. We both left that day with a better understanding of each other, as well as a feeling of having been blessed.

> *I have to admit that some people are just hard for me to be around.*

Loving Lord Jesus, thank you for modeling acceptance of "unacceptable" people during your life here on earth. Thank you for accepting me with all of my shortcomings and quirks. Please work in and through me to reach out to others. Help me to show your acceptance of them through how I relate to them in a spirit of acceptance. Amen.

87
Proclaim
His Praise

Mary K. Mohler

> But you are a chosen generation, a royal
> priesthood, a holy nation, His own special
> people, that you may proclaim the praises of
> Him who called you out of darkness into his
> marvelous light.

1 Peter 2:9 NKJV

God is so good to give us many clear, profound pictures of what our lives look like in him.
Think about the word pictures in 1 Peter 2:9 alone.
As New Testament believers, we are God's own special people. He literally called us out of a darkness
that knows no end and brought us into the brilliant
beams of his abiding and eternal light.

Sometimes we in ministry lose sight of how
awesome it is to be called to leadership among this
"chosen generation." We try so hard not to let our
guard down. We are supposed to be as solid as a rock.
We get so overwhelmed by all the responsibilities of
the day that our joy is overshadowed by fatigue or
overcommitment. Yet as ministry wives, we know

that we are constantly being watched by both Christians and non-Christians.

Consider this verse again. We are created to proclaim God's praises. It is terribly hard to do this when we are having a pity party. My friend, rest assured that your labor is not in vain. Yes, we are busy, but we must be busy doing the right things, so that our God-ordained purpose to proclaim God's praises is first and foremost.

> We know that we are constantly being watched by both Christians and non-Christians.

Blessed Father, thank you for loving us in spite of who we are. Thank you for giving us encouragement as no one else can through your Word and the power of the Holy Spirit. Lord, we want to walk as children of light and proclaim your praises forevermore. Give us the strength this day to do just that, wherever and however you choose to use us. In Jesus' name. Amen.

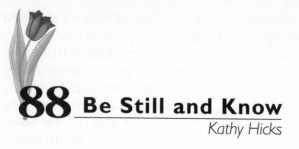

88 Be Still and Know
Kathy Hicks

Be still, and know that I am God.

Psalm 46:10

This verse always speaks to my soul. Maybe it's the hectic pace of life that makes the thought of being still and meditating on the "Godness" of God so appealing. One day as I was contemplating this verse I wondered, *"What does* being still *really mean? And just what does God want me to know about him?"* Here are some thoughts God spoke to my heart:

"Be still, and know that I am God."

Be calm and realize that I am in ultimate control of what touches your life. It is my love for you that motivates me as I work on your behalf.

Be quiet and listen to what I want to say to you. Allow me the chance to speak to your heart about what I'm doing in your life.

Be content and believe that I know what your needs are before you ask and that it gives me great pleasure to meet those needs—and even to give you the desires of your heart, as you delight yourself in me.

What may seem like unanswered prayer to you is really my perfect timing for you and for those in your life.

Be patient and realize that what I'm accomplishing in you and through you may take weeks, months, and even years to complete—so what may seem like unanswered prayer to you is really my perfect timing for you and for those in your life.

Be thankful because I am all-powerful, all-wise, loving, just, patient, and so much more. I am all these things on your behalf. You can trust me with your life.

"Be still, and know that I am God."

Father, quiet my heart so I can listen to yours. Muffle the distractions and show me what I need to understand about you today. Thank you for all that you are and all that you do on my behalf. Amen.

89 "That Feeling"

Joyce Webster

You have made known to me the path of life;
you will fill me with joy in your presence,
with eternal pleasures at your right hand.

Psalm 16:11

I get nervous when my husband gets "that feeling." Why? Because it usually means change. "That feeling" has caused moves from business to full-time ministry, from youth ministry to ministry as a senior pastor, and from a pastorate to mission work in Eastern Europe. Life is an adventure being married to this man. Yet, even more important, life is an adventure being God's child and following him on the path of life.

While in Austria Bob began to have "that feeling" again about Moscow. As was our family's custom, Bob asked each family member to pray about where God might be leading. Rachel, one of our daughters, responded candidly that she didn't want to pray about it because she knew God would "make us go to Moscow." She was convinced that praying would only lead to Moscow. Didn't God always lead believers to harder situations? We realized then that we had to tackle a bigger question than where we might serve.

The question now was, *What kind of people would we be?* Would we be people who put limits on our willingness to follow God, or people who say yes to God even before knowing the question? Rather than spending time praying about *where* we would go, we began praying about *who* we would be. At our next family meeting, we discovered that God had convinced each of us individually, and as a family, that we wanted to be people who said yes to God, no matter what the question. Saying yes to God didn't lead to Moscow in the end, but to the United States to plant a church.

> *Would we be people who put limits on our willingness to follow God, or people who say yes to God even before knowing the question?*

Following God down his path is not always comfortable, but I believe it is only on this "path of life" that I truly find joy and eternal pleasures!

Father, give me the courage to say yes to you even before I know the question. Fill me with anticipation for wherever the path of life will lead. Amen.

90 Praying for Your Husband

Lisa Ryken

> *Pray also for me, that whenever I open my mouth, words may be given me so that I will fearlessly make known the mystery of the gospel, for which I am an ambassador in chains. Pray that I may declare it fearlessly, as I should.*
>
> *Ephesians 6:19–20*

One of the most challenging sermons I've ever heard was based on this text from Ephesians, urging believers to pray for their preachers. The apostle Paul was a brilliant preacher and a bold evangelist, yet he recognized that, in order for his ministry to be effective, he needed people to pray for him. Preaching the gospel is a solemn task. To proclaim the Word of God a preacher needs words from God, so that he will depend on God's Word and not on his own skill. He needs the freedom and boldness to proclaim the gospel fearlessly, not telling people what they want to hear but what God wants them to hear. A preacher must proclaim the mystery of the gospel, not a carefully calculated plan for moral improvement. He must make sinners uncomfortable with their sin and point them to Jesus Christ. Finally, ministers need endurance in tribulation. They need to bear the burdens of their congregation as they stay tender to the pain of sin.

I realized how much I need to pray for my husband and how little I actually did pray for him.

By the end of the sermon I was in tears. I realized how much I need to pray for my husband and how little I actually did pray for him. Even more than that, I felt the weight of his burden to preach the gospel. As his wife I must bear that burden with him and pray for him faithfully.

Lord, thank you for faithful preachers who open your Word to us plainly. Thank you for my husband and his gift for proclaiming the gospel. Please give him boldness and endurance. Please forgive me for praying infrequently and weakly. Equip me to be his constant prayer warrior. Amen.

Contributors

Kathy Chapell

Kathy and Bryan Chapell serve the Lord at Covenant Theological Seminary, where Bryan is the president. The Chapells have four children, ranging in age from 19 to 7. Kathy holds bachelor's and master's degrees in music education and performance and has served as music director in several churches, most recently at Covenant Presbyterian Church in St. Louis, Missouri.

Jeanne Hendricks

Based on her many years as a partner in ministry with her husband, Howard, professor at Dallas Theological Seminary, Jeanne is a writer and speaker for pastors' wives and women's ministries. She maintains discipleship and counseling with young women and is the mother of three grown children and grandmother of six.

Kathy Hicks

Kathy Hicks has been involved in ministry with her husband, Rick, since 1975. Previously at Forest Home Christian Conference Center in California, they are now serving Operation Mobilization, a mission agency whose United States headquarters is in Atlanta, Georgia. She enjoys her role as wife of the president of OM USA and enlistment advisor. Kathy also serves on the board of the Finishers Project and has coauthored a book with her husband on generational differences, a topic on which they often teach together. They have a daughter, Cora, who is in college.

Barbara Hughes

Barbara Hughes serves the Lord as a homemaker, pastor's wife, and grandmother. She has coauthored two books with her husband, Kent Hughes. Her most recent book, *Disciplines of a Godly Woman* (Crossway), calls on women to bring every area of their lives into submission to God's will. Barbara and Kent serve and worship the Lord at College Church in Wheaton, Illinois, and have four grown children and sixteen grandchildren.

Mary Kassian

Mary Kassian is a Canadian author, speaker, and president of Alabaster Flask Ministries, an organization that challenges young women to love God extravagantly and to joyfully embrace his design for them. Her husband, Brent, is chaplain for the local professional football team. Mary and Brent along with their three sons live in Sherwood Park, Alberta, Canada, where they enjoy biking, hiking, mountains, campfires, hockey, and their children's black lab, General Beau.

Mary K. Mohler

Mary K. Mohler serves in ministry as the president's wife at The Southern Baptist Theological Seminary in Louisville, Kentucky, and as the founder and director of the Seminary Wives Institute. Her favorite role is that of homemaker for her husband, Albert, and their two children, Katie and Christopher. Mary is a native of suburban Detroit, Michigan, and is a summa cum laude graduate of Samford University.

Heather Olford

Heather Olford—pastor's wife, mother of two, and gifted pianist—makes her home in Memphis, Tennessee. Born in Lurgan, Northern Ireland, she has served alongside her famous husband, Dr. Stephen Olford, in two metropolitan churches—one in London, England, the other in New York City. In both churches she was involved in counseling, women's work, and music. Presently they conduct preaching seminars and workshops at the Stephen Olford Center for Biblical Preaching in Memphis, as well as at other centers worldwide. She and Stephen have two sons.

Jani Ortlund

Jani Ortlund is an author and conference speaker for Renewal Ministries. Her recent book *Fearlessly Feminine* (Multnomah) encourages women to boldly embrace God's design for them as women. Jan is married to Dr. Ray Ortlund Jr., senior pastor of the historic First Presbyterian Church of Augusta, Georgia. The Ortlunds have four grown children.

Dorothy Kelley Patterson

Dorothy Kelley Patterson resides in North Carolina with her husband, Paige Patterson, the president of Southeastern Baptist Theological Seminary and the former president of the Southern Baptist Convention. She describes herself as a homemaker, a task that has always commanded her priority in time, energies, and creativity. Dr. Patterson is a well-respected free-lance writer and speaker. Currently she is assistant professor of women's studies at Southeastern Baptist Seminary. She is the author of *BeAttitudes for Women* (Broadman), *A Woman Seeking God* (Broadman), and *Where's Mom?* (Council for Biblical Manhood and Womanhood).

Noël Piper

Since 1980, Noël Piper and her husband, John, have served in ministry at Bethlehem Baptist Church in Minneapolis, Minnesota. She enjoys speaking and writing and is grateful for each opportunity for mission-related travel. But her main calling is to her family. She and John have four sons and a daughter.

Lisa Ryken

Elisabeth (Lisa) Maxwell Ryken graduated from Wheaton College, Wheaton, Illinois (Bachelor of Arts, History), and Arcadia University, Glenside, Pennsylvania (Master of Arts,

Education). She currently worships and serves at Tenth Presbyterian Church in Philadelphia, Pennsylvania, where her husband, Philip, is the senior minister. The Rykens live in Center City Philadelphia with their three children, Joshua, Kirsten, and James.

Sue Sailhamar

Sue Sailhamer served as a pastor's wife for twenty-four years. Her husband, Paul, was the senior associate at the First Evangelical Free Church of Fullerton, California. He is now president of a private Christian foundation. Sue serves as "mentor mom" for the MOPS (Mothers of Preschoolers, International) ministry at the Fullerton church and writes for the Southern California *Christian Times*. The Sailhamers have two grown sons and one daughter-in-law.

Paulette Washington

Paulette Washington has served as a pastor's wife (husband, Raleigh) at the Rock of Our Salvation Church in Chicago, Illinois, for many years, followed by ministry with Promise Keepers. She is a graduate of Fayetteville State University in North Carolina where she earned her teacher's credentials. Paulette is founder of Harvest Evangelistic Outreach and president of Reconciliation and Peace Ministries, Inc. She is a popular speaker at conferences for youth and women, as well as at conferences on marriage and family issues.

Joyce Webster

Joyce Webster has served as a pastor's wife, schoolteacher, and missionary to Eastern Europe. Currently she teaches fifth grade at Pasadena Christian School. In 1997 Joyce and her husband, Bob, planted Foothills Community Church in Pasadena, California, where they continue to serve. The Websters have five grown children.

Mary Lou Whitlock

Mary Lou Whitlock has served the Lord alongside her husband, Luder, in the church and in the academic world. Early in their ministry, Luder pastored churches and then became president of Reformed Theological Seminary in Orlando, Florida. Recently retired, they are active in pro-family programs, as well as in programs for wives of seminary students (Mrs. In Ministry). They have three married children (Chris, Alissa, Beth) and nine grandchildren.

Scripture Index

We want to hear from you. Please send your comments about this book to us in care of zreview@zondervan.com. Thank you.

GRAND RAPIDS, MICHIGAN 49530 USA

WWW.ZONDERVAN.COM